SECOND EDITION

Write from the Start

David M. Davidson
Bronx Community College
City University of New York

David Blot
Bronx Community College
City University of New York

HEINLE & HEINLE PUBLISHERS
A Division of Wadsworth, Inc.
Boston, MA 02116

The publication of *Write from the Start, Second Edition,* was directed by the members of the Newbury House Publishing Team at Heinle & Heinle:

Erik Gundersen, Editorial Director
John McHugh, Market Development Director
Gabrielle B. McDonald, Production Editor

Also participating in the publication of this program were:

Publisher: Stanley J. Galek
Editorial Production Manager: Elizabeth Holthaus
Project Manager: Ros Herion Freese
Assistant Editor: Karen P. Hazar
Associate Marketing Manager: Donna Hamilton
Production Assistant: Maryellen Eschmann
Manufacturing Coordinator: Mary Beth Hennebury
Illustrator: Theresa Troise Heidel
Interior Designer: Ros Herion Freese
Cover Designer: Bortman Design Group

Photo Credits: p. 8 right: Mimi Forsyth / Monkmeyer Press. pp. 8 left, 28, and 41: Ulrike Welsch Photography. pp. 9, 80 left, and 99: David Frasier Photolibrary. p. 10: Mary Kate Denny / PhotoEdit. p. 17: Gary Conner / PhotoEdit. p. 22 right: Peter Keegan / FPG International. p. 22 left: James Carroll / Stock Boston. pp. 38 and 96: David Young-Wolff / PhotoEdit. p. 30: Jerry Berndt / Stock Boston. p. 35: Ros Herion Freese. p. 42: Bachmann / The Image Works. p. 63: FPG International. p. 68: Michael Lajoie Photography. p. 76: Voller Ernst / The Image Works. p. 80 right: Arlene Collins / Monkmeyer Press. p. 81: Felicia Martinez / PhotoEdit. p. 103: Comstock, Inc. p. 108: Cleo Photography / PhotoEdit. p. 111: Michael Newman / PhotoEdit.

Heinle & Heinle Publishers is a division of Wadsworth, Inc.

Manufactured in the United States of America

Library of Congress Cataloging in Publication Data

Davidson, David M.
    Write from the Start.

    1. English language—Text-books for foreign speakers.
    2. English language—Composition and exercises.
    I. Blot, Dave. II. Title
    PE1128.D348   1994   808'.042   93-43511

ISBN: 0-8384-4848-8

10 9 8 7 6 5 4 3 2

Contents

SECTION FOUR   TELLING STORIES   69

SECTION FIVE   PUTTING AN END TO IT   77

SECTION SIX   EXERCISING   83

SECTION SEVEN   GRAMMAR STUDY AND PRACTICE   123

Introduction

This second edition of *Write from the Start*, 10 years and some 80,000 copies after its original publication, undertakes the risk of trying to improve on a good thing. What is "good" about *WFTS* is that it has lived up to the claim, suggested by its punny title and proclaimed by its then young and confident authors, that "beginning adult ESL learners can write English, given proper guidance and security."

Now, not quite as young but ever confident, we reiterate the principles stated in the first edition.

1. Students benefit from the opportunity to express their ideas orally before writing them.
2. Students will be more willing to express themselves through speaking and writing (i.e., to take the risks involved) if they really want to communicate.
3. Once they have invested themselves in communicating through writing, students will be ready and motivated to learn the technicalities of grammar, spelling, and so on.

Write from the Start was therefore structured to help instructors provide their students with the security and opportunities to become confident users of written and spoken English. It does this by providing activities that

1. immediately engage students in speaking and writing,
2. are both controlled enough to provide security and interesting enough for adults to want to be bothered with,
3. encourage student interaction, and
4. provide experience and practice in the basics of English.

Most of what we presented in the first edition achieved our objectives. Some did not. Seizing the opportunity of this second edition to produce an even better text, we have revised or eliminated those exercises that proved difficult or ineffective, and we have provided more of what worked: an expanded first section that is both the jumping-off point and the heart of the book, and more and varied grammar exercises in the last two sections.

Section One, **Starting to Write,** provides the control, guidance, security, and opportunity for students to talk and write about themselves, their friends, their relatives, and their ideas. The last two sections, **Exercising** and **Grammar Study and Practice,** employ a variety of formats we have found useful in giving students practice in some of the basics. These sections are placed last because we feel they should be used after students have attempted to function in the language and after the instructor has responded to their interests and needs by teaching discrete grammatical points. Students will learn to write by writing. The teaching will be more appropriate and effective when it responds to the needs of the students as they perceive them through their desire to communicate effectively.

Activities from the sections in between are intended to be used interchangeably at the instructor's discretion, depending on the students' level, rate of progress, and needs.

Users of the first edition will note in **Starting to Write:** tighter grammatical control, more logical paragraph development, and more opportunities for students to work with the simple future and present continuous tenses. The **Filling In** exercises have been made more accessible by better layout and control of choices; and new photographs of higher quality but of equally engaging content have been incorporated throughout.

We trust this second edition will be interesting and fun for both students and teachers, the kind of textbook that people want to turn to. If our intention has been realized, students will learn from it and teachers will enjoy helping them use it.

THE SECTIONS

Section One, **Starting to Write,** is composed of three different types of exercises organized by tense in order of difficulty. The simplest type of exercise is the *model composition* (*My Classmate, About Me,* and *A Good Friend* in the present tense; *My Parents, More About Me,* and *My Grandmother's House* in the past tense; *Next Weekend* in the future and *A Letter* in the present continuous). Students begin the activity by reading the questions to themselves and asking for help as they need it from the instructor or the other students. Then, in pairs or in small groups, they should ask each other the questions and take notes (where appropriate). They will then be asked to read the model composition (aloud or to themselves) and to write. The model provides considerable security in the form of structure and vocabulary for those who need it. Such students may need to copy the composition and substitute appropriate information. Those who have the ability to write without copying, or even without using the model, should be encouraged to do so.

The second type of exercise in this section asks students to move from *an oral to a writing activity.* (*Getting to Know You, Twins,* and *The Storekeeper* in the present; *The Park, An Evening Out, The Phone Call, The Test,* and *The First Day of English Class* in the past; and *A Trip Together* in the future). The questions on the left-hand page (Activity A) are intended for oral use by students in pairs or groups. Their purpose is to have students think and talk about the topic and to structure their responses orally before getting to the writing. The questions on the right-hand page (Activity B, etc.) provide considerable security for those who need it. Students may choose from among the possibilities offered or supply their own information. Again, those with more facility should be encouraged to write their own stories, using the questions only as an outline.

All of the remaining activities in this section call for *responses to questions,* some highly structured with choices, some more open-ended, and some supported by illustrations. Most of them suggest beginning with a discussion which in most cases is about a third person—friend, teacher, parent, or relative. These exercises tend to be longer, offer some guidance as to paragraph division, and in some cases involve writing in more than one tense. Where the person is imaginary (e.g., Donald in *A Vacation,* Nancy in *The Illness,* and Peter in *A Decision*), the partners must agree on the details to be written.

Section One, along with the exercise work in the back and any supplementary work and instruction provided by the teacher, could well compose a third to a half or more of a semester's work, depending upon the level and rate of development of the students. Where some students develop their writing ability at a much faster pace than others, they of course may be encouraged to move ahead in the book to the other sections.

The order of exercises in this section does not necessarily suggest the teacher's order of pre-sentation. For example, many teachers prefer to begin with the past tense, and it is often useful to return to a tense exercise for review.

Aside from being fun, the **Filling In** exercises (Section Two) are designed to give students some awareness of grammatical forms and sentence structure as well as some vocabulary extension. Activity A, word selection, is excellent for group work. Activity B, follow-up copying and/or writing, is an individual activity. In the former, any choice of words or phrases should be acceptable if they are grammatically and semantically appropriate to the context.

In our first book for more advanced students, *Put It In Writing,* we found dialogue activities to be very popular with students because the situations involved them in realistic conflicts they could identify with, yet permitted them the distance and security of role-playing. The dialogue situations in Section Three, **Talking It Over,** are intended to be fairly common experiences which nevertheless generate emotion and which can be dealt with in relatively simple, familiar language. This type of exercise should be demonstrated by a dialogue either between a teacher and a student or between two students. (In pairing students for this activity we found that, as a rule, women feel more comfortable playing male roles than vice versa, so dialogues calling for male–female interaction should be conducted by a male and a female or by two females. Of course, you can change the gender of a character if you feel that is more appropriate.)

In Section Four, **Telling Stories,** students are given the opportunity to write in more than one tense or to choose between present and past. The directions are clear, and once again we urge that discussion precede writing.

Students must write in the past tense to complete the stories in Section Five, **Putting an End to It.** The person and tone vary from story to story, however, providing the opportunity for a range of writing experiences.

As we stated earlier, "teaching" should follow "doing," and so we regard Section Six, **Exercising,** as supplementary to the writing activities in the rest of the book. We use the fill-in story format because it allows students to practice major grammatical points while building a story. In a second format in this section, students must produce questions for given answers. Walk the students through a couple of the earlier exercises, especially the *questions for answers.* Having to provide questions for answers, the reverse of the normal language function, will require patient training at first. But after a few exercises, most students will understand how to do it. We have found this format, in spite of its unnaturalness, to be highly stimulating—an effective teaching device that helps students make connections between the wording of questions and answers, and that forces them to respond to the content of the accompanying stories.

Finally, for this new edition, we have added Section Seven, **Grammar Study and Practice**—exercises for a selected group of grammatical items that beginning students will find most useful.

We have enjoyed writing this book, and our students have enjoyed using it while making significant and satisfying progress in developing their language skills. We hope you and your students have similar experiences and we invite you to share them with us.

David M. Davidson
David Blot

SECTION ONE

Starting to Write

My Classmate

ACTIVITY   Get to know your classmate. Ask your classmate the questions below. Write the answers on a piece of paper. Then your classmate will ask you the questions and will write the answers.

1. What is your name?
2. Where are you from?
3. How old are you?
4. Where do you live?
5. Who do you live with?
6. Do you have any brothers and sisters?
7. Are you married?
8. Do you have any children?
9. Why are you studying English?
10. What do you like to do in your free time?

Now write a paragraph about your classmate. First read the paragraph below. You may use it as a model if you want to.

My Classmate

My classmate's name is Elizabeth. She is from Greece. She is 22 years old. She lives in Westwood with her mother, father, and three sisters. Elizabeth is not married. She doesn't have any children, but she wants to have a son and a daughter. She is studying English because she wants to be a computer programmer. In her free time Elizabeth likes to play tennis, read good books, and go out with her friends. She wants me to play tennis with her on Saturday. I'm happy that Elizabeth is my classmate.

The Interview

ACTIVITY A   Choose a new partner. Ask your partner the following questions. Write the answers on the form below.

1. What is your last name?   2. What is your first name?   3. What is your middle initial?
4. What is your address?   5. What is your phone number?
6. When were you born?   7. Where were you born?
8. What is your father's name?   9. What is your mother's name?
10. When did you arrive in ~~the United States~~? *Canada?*
11. Why are you going to this school?
~~12. What is your curriculum or major?~~
13. What do you want to do when you finish school?
14. What languages do you speak?
15. What are your hobbies and interests?

Student Interview Form

1. _____   2. _____   3. _____
   Last Name   First Name   Middle Initial

4. _____   5. ( )_____
   Address: Number, Street, ~~State~~ *Prov,* ~~Zip Code~~   (Area Code) Phone Number
                                      Postal Code

6. _____   7. _____
   Date of Birth   Place of Birth

8. Father—_____   9. Mother—_____
                       Parents' Names

10. _____
    Date of Arrival in ~~the U.S.A.~~ *Canada*

11. _____
    Reasons for choosing this school

~~12.~~ _____
    ~~Curriculum (Major Subject)~~

13. _____
    Career Goals

14. _____
    Languages Spoken

15. _____
    Hobbies, Interests, etc.

                                            _____
                                            Signature of Interviewer

ACTIVITY B   Write a brief description of the person you interviewed.

I interviewed _____ ___. _____.

He/She lives at_____.

He/She was born on _____ ___, _____ in _____.
                           (Date)   (Country)

His/Her father's name is _____ and

his/her mother's name is _____.

_____ arrived in ~~the United States~~ on _____ ___, _____.
        (First name)   *Canada*

He/She is going to _____ because
                       (name of this school)

_____.

_____ ~~curriculum or major is~~ _____.
~~(His/Her)~~

When _____ finishes school, _____ wants to _____.
         (first name)   (he/she)

_____.

_____ speaks _____.
   (First name)   (languages)

_____ likes to _____.

_____.

_____.

About Me

ACTIVITY Choose someone in the class that you don't know very well. Ask this person the following questions. Then your partner will ask you the questions. Write *your* answers about *yourself.*

1. What is your name?
2. How old are you?
3. Where do you come from?
4. Where do you live?
5. Who do you live with?
6. Are your parents and brothers and sisters here or in your native country?
7. What is your major subject in school?
   or
   What kind of job do you have?
8. What do you want to do in the future?
9. What are your hobbies?
10. Is there anything else you want to tell about yourself?

Now write a paragraph about yourself. First read the paragraph below. You may use it as a model if you want to.

About Me

My name is Tom. I am 23 years old. I come from Cambodia. I live at 193 Union Avenue. I live with my brother and his wife. My parents are in Cambodia. I have another brother and two sisters in Cambodia, also. My major subject is Electrical Technology. I want to become an engineer. My hobbies are dancing and going to the movies. After I finish my education, I want to get a good job. I also want to get married and have children.

A Good Friend

ACTIVITY   Ask your partner or someone in your group these questions. Then your partner or someone in your group will ask you the questions. Write your answers about your friend.

1. What is your friend's name?
2. What nationality is your friend?
3. How old is your friend?
4. How tall is your friend?
5. How much does your friend weigh?
6. What color is your friend's hair?
7. What color are your friend's eyes?
8. Is your friend's complexion light or dark?
9. What clothes does your friend wear?
10. Is your friend intelligent? Understanding? Generous?
11. Does your friend have a good sense of humor?
12. What is the most important thing you want to tell about your friend?

Now write a paragraph about your friend. First read the paragraph below. You may use it as a model if you want to.

A Good Friend

My friend's name is Marie. She is Haitian. She is 20 years old. Marie is 5' 3" tall and weighs about 110 pounds. Her hair is black and her eyes are brown. She has a dark complexion. She usually wears a skirt and sweater to school. She wears jeans at home. Marie is very intelligent and very understanding. She has a good sense of humor. She always laughs at my jokes. Marie is a good athlete. She likes sports. She also likes music and children. We get along very well together.

Getting to Know You

ACTIVITY A   Ask your partner these questions. Then your partner will ask you the questions. Write *your* answers to the questions about *you* on a separate piece of paper.

1. What do you like to do for entertainment?
    Go to movies, shows, museums, concerts, sports events, _____?

2. What physical activities do you like to do?
    Swim?   Jog?   Ride a bicycle?   Play baseball?   Play tennis?
    _____?

3. What other activities do you like?
    Parties?   Dances?   Eating in restaurants?
    Drinking?   Gambling?   Traveling?   Reading?   Watching television?
    _____?

4. Is there anything else you especially like to do?
    Paint?   Write?   Sing?
    Play an instrument?
    Collect stamps, baseball cards, _____?
    _____?

5. What food do you like?   What food do you dislike?

6. What are the most important things in life for you?
    Religion?   Money?   Love?
    _____?

7. What do you want to do in the future?
    Have children?   Become famous?
    Become a professional?
    Go back to your native country?
    _____?

8

ACTIVITY B   Write a story about your partner. Write it on a separate piece of paper. It should look like this:

_____
(Your Partner's Name)

I have a classmate named _____. He/She likes to
_____
_____
_____

1. Does _____ like to go to *movies?*
                                                shows?
                                                museums?
                                                concerts?
                                                sports events?
                                                _____?

2. Does he/she like to *swim?*
                        jog?
                        ride a bicycle?   3. *Does* he/she like *parties?*
                        play baseball?   *dances?*
                        play tennis?   *eating in restaurants?*
                                                                          drinking
                        _____?   *gambling?*
                                                                          traveling?
                                                                          reading?
                                                                          watching television?

                                                                          _____

4. Does _____ especially like to *paint?*
                                              write?
                                              sing?
                                              play an instrument?
                                              collect stamps?
                                              collect baseball cards?

                                              _____?

                        5. Does he/she like *Chinese food?*
                                            Spanish food?
                                            American food?
                                            vegetables?
                                            ice cream? _____?

                        6. Is *religion* very important to _____?
                              money
                              love

                              _____

                        7. Does he/she want to *have children?*
                                               become famous?
                                               become a professional?
                                               go back to live in his/her native country?

Twins

ACTIVITY A   Ask your partner or someone in your group these questions. Then your partner or someone in your group will ask you the questions.

1. Do you know twins? What are their names? Do they look exactly alike, or can you tell them apart?

2. How old are they?

3. Who do they live with?

4. What do they do?

5. Do they like to do the same things or different things? Give examples.

6. Do you like them? Why or why not?

7. Do they like each other, or do they fight a lot?

8. Are they good to their parents? friends? children?

9. Are they happy or unhappy? Explain.

ACTIVITY B   Write a story about the twins, Anna and Maria, on a separate piece of paper. Write one paragraph. Your paragraph should look like this:

Twins

Anna and Maria look exactly like each other. They _____

_____

_____

_____

_____

_____

1. Do Anna and Maria look *exactly like each other?*
    a little like each other?
    different from each other?

2. Are they *children?*
    teenagers?
    adults?

    _____?

3. Do they live *with their parents?*
    with their husbands and children?
    alone?

    _____?

4. Do they *go to school?*
    work?

    _____?

5. Do they like the same *clothes?*
    books?
    games?
    friends?

    _____?

6. Are they *funny?*
    interesting?
    selfish?
    generous?

    _____?

7. Are they good to each other?

8. Are they good to their *parents?*
    friends?
    children?

9. Are they happy or unhappy? Explain.

ACTIVITY C   Write a short composition about the following:

1. Is it good to be a twin?   2.   What is the best way to raise or treat twins?

The Storekeeper

ACTIVITY A   Ask your partner or someone in your group these questions. Then your partner or someone in your group will ask you the questions.

1. Do you shop in a small store in your neighborhood?

2. Who is the owner of the store?

3. Where is the store located?

4. What time does the store open each day?

5. Do many people come to the store every day?

6. Why do you like to go there? Is it convenient? Inexpensive? Open early or late?

7. What kind of person is the storekeeper? Is he or she friendly? Courteous? Generous? Bad-tempered? Neat? Sloppy?

8. Do you like him or her? Why?

9. What time does the store close each day?

ACTIVITY B   On a separate piece of paper, write a story about Mr. Caruso. Write three paragraphs. Your composition should look like this:

The Storekeeper

Mr. Caruso is the owner of a _____.

The store _____

_____.

Many people _____

_____

_____.

Mr. Caruso _____

_____

_____.

1st para.
Is Mr. Caruso the owner of *a grocery store?   a candy store?*
a discount store?
_____?

Is the store *across the street from the movie theater?   next to the post office?*
around the corner from the dry cleaners?
_____?

Does Mr. Caruso open his store every morning *at 7:00?   at 8:00?   at 9:00?*
at _____?

Does he get everything ready for business?
Then does he begin to wait on the customers?

2nd para.
Do many people come to his store every day?
Do they shop there *because it is convenient?*
because his prices are reasonable?
because it is the only store nearby?
because _____?
Do the customers like Mr. Caruso? Why or why not?

3rd para.
Does Mr. Caruso close his store *at 5:00?   at 6:00?   at 9:30?*
at _____?
After work, is he *very happy?   very tired?   very sleepy?* } Why?
very _____?

A Vacation

ACTIVITY   Donald is a friend of yours. With your partner, talk about Donald's vacation.
Using the choices you are given, you and your partner decide what you want to write. Then
write three paragraphs. Each of you write on your own paper.

1st para.

Does Donald take his vacation in *July* every year?
                                            August
                                            December

_____

Does he usually go to *Hawaii?*
                       Puerto Rico?
                       France?

_____?

Does he travel alone? Why or why not?

2nd para.

Does he like *the beaches?*
             the night life?
             the food?

_____?

Does he like the people? Why or why not?
During the day does he *swim at the beach?*
                       get a suntan?
                       relax by the swimming pool?
                       play golf?

_____?

In the evening does he *dance in a discotheque?*
                       gamble in a casino?
                       have a quiet dinner with a friend?

_____?

3rd para.

Does Donald spend a lot of money on his vacation?
At the end of his vacation does he want to return home? Why or why not?

The Teacher

ACTIVITY With your partner, talk about one of your teachers. Using the choices you are given, you and your partner decide what you want to write. Then write four paragraphs. Each of you write on your own paper.

1st para.

When your teacher comes to class, does he/she *say "hello" to everyone?*
put his/her books on the desk?
take off his/her coat?
_____?

Does he/she tell the students *to get ready for class?*
to hand in the homework?
to stop talking?
to _____?

Does he/she take attendance?

2nd para.

When the class is ready to begin, does the teacher explain what you are going to do during the class?
Then does he/she usually *teach a lesson at the blackboard?*
give you an activity to do?
give you an assignment in your book?
_____?

Does he/she answer your questions while you are working in class?

3rd para.

Is the class *easy?*
hard? } Why?
just right?

Do the students pay attention to the teacher? Why or why not?

Do the students usually *work together as a whole class?*
work together in small groups?
_____?

4th para.

Is your teacher *a funny person?*
a serious person?
a happy person?
a friendly person?
a _____?

Are you happy that you are a student in his/her class? Why or why not?

Another Good Friend

ACTIVITY   Tell your partner or your group about a good friend. Then write about your friend. Write three paragraphs.

1st para.   What is your friend's name?
Is your friend married or single?
Does your friend have any children?
Where does your friend live?

2nd para.   Does your friend work? Where? What does your friend do?
Does your friend go to school? Where? What is your friend's curriculum?
On weekends, does your friend like to *go to dances?*
go to parties?
go out on dates?
go out with the family?
stay home and watch TV?
_____?

3rd para.   Does your friend have a happy life? Why or why not?
Why is he or she a good friend?

A Holiday in My Country

ACTIVITY   With your partner or your group talk about a holiday in your country that is not a holiday in the United States.   Then write about this holiday.   Write three paragraphs.

1st para.
What is the name of the holiday?
On what day or days do the people of your country celebrate it?
Is it a religious holiday or a political holiday or some other kind of holiday?

2nd para.
What do the people do on this holiday?
　　Do they have a parade?
　　Do they dance in the streets?
　　Do they wear special clothes?
　　Do they cook a lot of food for friends and neighbors?
　　Do they stay at home and pray?

3rd para.   Why is this holiday important for the people of your country?

My Parents

ACTIVITY   Ask your partner or someone in your group the following questions. Then your partner or someone in your group will ask you the questions. Write *your* answers about *your* parents.

1. Where was your mother born?
2. Where was your father born?
3. When were they born?
4. Did they go to school? Where?
5. How long did they go to school?
6. Did they have brothers and sisters?
7. Did they live with their parents or with some other relatives?

Now write a paragraph about your parents. First read the paragraph below. You may use it as a model if you want to.

My Parents

My mother was born in San Juan, Puerto Rico in 1944. My father was born in Ponce, but I don't know when. My mother went to elementary school and then to Colegio San Juan. She finished high school. My father went to school in Ponce until the eighth grade. He didn't finish school because he had to help take care of his family. My mother had two brothers and two sisters. She lived with her parents. My father had three sisters and one brother. He lived with his parents until he was 14 years old. Then his father died and he went to live with an uncle. He worked in his uncle's store to help support his family.

More About Me

ACTIVITY   Ask your partner or someone in your group the following questions. Then your partner or someone in your group will ask you the questions. Write *your* answers about *yourself*.

1. Where were you born?
2. When were you born?
3. What did your father do?
4. What did your mother do?
5. Did you go to elementary school? Where?
6. Did you like school? Why or why not?
7. Did you go to high school? If yes, where? If no, why not?
8. When did you come to the United States?
9. Where do you live now?
10. Do you miss your country? Why or why not?
11. Are you happy to be in the United States? Why or why not?

Now write a paragraph about yourself. First read the paragraph below. You may use it as a model if you want to.

More About Me

I was born in Vietnam in 1980. I grew up in a small village. My father was a farmer. My mother took care of me and my brothers and sisters. I went to elementary school in my village. I liked school because I made many friends. I didn't go to high school because I had to help my father. When I was 19, I left Vietnam with my brother and came to the United States. Now we live in Portland, Oregon. I miss my country because all my friends and family are there. I am happy to be in the United States because life is easier and I have more opportunities for an education and a good future.

My Grandmother's House

ACTIVITY   Ask your partner the following questions. Then your partner will ask you the questions. Write *your* answers about *yourself*.

1. When you were a child, did you like to visit the house of a special relative?
2. Where did she/he live?
3. What color was the house?
4. How many rooms did it have?
5. What was your favorite place in the house? Why?
6. What important things did you learn from this relative?

Now write a composition about this house and your relative. First read the paragraph below. You may use it as a model.

My Grandmother's House

When I was a child, I used to visit my grandmother's house. She lived outside the city on a small farm.

My grandmother's house was painted pink and blue. It had a porch in the front and in the back. The house had seven rooms, three bedrooms, a living room, a dining room, a kitchen, and a bathroom.

My favorite place was the yard because it was big and there were many animals. My grandmother raised chickens, ducks, turkeys, and pigs, and she had a cow and a horse. She also had a vegetable garden where she planted tomatoes, carrots, and beets.

I learned from my grandmother that all living things—people, animals, and plants—can be beautiful and need attention. I will never forget my grandmother's house and the things I learned there.

The Illness

ACTIVITY   With your partner talk about Nancy and her daughter or son. Using the choices you are given, you and your partner decide what you want to write. Then write two paragraphs. Each of you write on your own paper.

1st para.

Did Nancy take her ⎰ *daughter* ⎱ to the *hospital?*
⎱ *son* ⎰   *clinic?*
                          doctor?
                          dentist?

_____?

Did her ⎰ *daughter* ⎱ have *a cold?*
⎱ *son* ⎰   *the flu?*
                      a cut on the leg?
                      a toothache?

_____?

Were there *many people* in the waiting room?
        only a few people

_____

Did Nancy have to wait *a long time?*
                an hour?
                only a few minutes?
                only a short time?

_____?

2nd para.

Did the *doctor* examine her ⎰ *daughter?*
        dentist   ⎱ *son?*

_____

Did her ⎰ *daughter* ⎱ cry? Why or why not?
⎱ *son* ⎰

Did the *doctor*   ⎰ *prescribe some medicine?*
        dentist   *give her/him an injection?*
        _____   ⎰ *put a bandage on the cut?*
                                      ⎱ *fill a cavity?*

Did the *doctor* tell Nancy   *to get the medicine right away?*
        dentist   *to come back in one week?*
        _____   *to call the next day?*
                                    to _____?

The next day did her ⎰ *daughter* ⎱ feel   *better?*
Two days later   ⎱ *son* ⎰   *worse?*
_____   *the same?*

_____?

21

The Park

ACTIVITY A   Ask your partner or someone in your group these questions. Then your partner or someone in your group will ask you the questions.

1. When did you last go to the park?

2. Who did you go with?

3. What kind of day was it?

4. What did you do?

5. Did you have anything to eat or drink? What?

6. How long did you stay?

7. Did you have a good time?

ACTIVITY B   On a separate piece of paper, write a story about the park. Write one paragraph. Begin like this:

The Park

Last _____ I went to _____ Park. _____

_____.

1. Last *Sunday* did you go to _____ Park?
    Saturday   (name of park)
    week

    _____

2. Did you go with *your family?*   *a friend?*   *alone?*_____?

3. Was it *a nice day?*
    a warm day?
    a cool day?
    a windy day?

    _____?

4. Did you *play ball?*
    go swimming in the pool?
    go rowing on the lake?
    relax on a blanket?
    jog around the lake?

    _____?

5. Did you bring food with you, or
    did you buy food in the park?

5a. Did you eat *hot dogs and*
    hamburgers?
    fried chicken?
    salad?
    sandwiches?

6. Did you spend *the whole day in the park?*
    the whole afternoon in the park?
    three hours in the park?

    _____?   _____?

7. When you went home, did you feel *tired?*   *happy?*   *sad?*   *relaxed?* }
    _____? } Why?

ACTIVITY C   Write a short composition about the following:

1. Do you enjoy going to the park? Why or why not?
2. What is your favorite park? Why?

An Evening Out

ACTIVITY A   Ask your partner or someone in your group these questions. Then your partner or someone in your group will ask you the questions.

1. When was your last date?

2. Who did you go out with?

3. How did you feel before the date?

4. Where did you go?

5. What did you do?

6. Did you have a good time?

7. Did you want to go out with this person again? Why or why not?

ACTIVITY B   On a separate piece of paper, write a story about a date. Write your story in three paragraphs. Your story should look like this:

An Evening Out

Last night I went out with _____. _____

_____.

We went _____

_____.

I wanted _____

_____.

1st para.
> Last *night* did you go out with your *friend?*
>   *Friday*   *husband?*
>   *Saturday*   *wife?*
>
> _____   _____?
>
> Before you went out were you *nervous?*
>   *excited?*   } Why?
>   *happy?*
>   _____?

2nd para.
> Did you go *out to dinner?*
>   *to the movies?*
>   *to a show?*
>   *dancing?*
>
>   _____?
>
> Were you *comfortable* with _____? Why?
>   *uncomfortable*   (name of person)
>
>   _____
>
> Did you enjoy *the dinner?*
>   *dancing?*   } Why or why not?
>   _____?
>
> Later, did you *walk around for a while?*
>   *get something to eat?*
>   *go to a bar for drinks?*
>   *go home together?*
>
>   _____?

3rd para.
> Did you want to go out with _____ again? Why?

ACTIVITY C   Write a short composition about the following: Do you like to go out on dates? Why or why not?

The Phone Call

ACTIVITY A   Ask your partner or someone in your group these questions. Then your partner or someone in your group will ask you the questions.

1. When did you last receive a phone call from someone you didn't want to talk to?

2. Who called you?

3. Were you surprised to hear from him/her? Why?

4. What did he/she want?

5. What did you tell him/her?

6. Did he/she get angry at you? Why or why not?

7. After the phone call, how did you feel? Why?

ACTIVITY B   Write a story about an unpleasant phone call that you received. Write three paragraphs.

1st para.
> *Last night* did your *ex-husband* call you?
> *Yesterday*   *ex-wife*
> *This morning*   *ex-boyfriend*
> _____   *ex-girlfriend*
>
> _____
>
> Were you surprised to hear from him/her? Why?

2nd para.
> Did he/she tell you that he/she wanted *to visit you?*
> *to invite you out?*
> *to discuss a problem?*
> *to borrow some money?*
>
> *to* _____?
>
> Did you tell him/her that you *didn't want to see him/her?*
> *didn't want to go out with him/her?*
> *didn't have time to talk?*
> *didn't have any money?*
>
> *didn't* _____?
>
> Did he/she get angry at you? Why or why not?
> Did you tell him/her *not to call you anymore?*
> *not to bother you anymore?*
> *to call you next week?*
>
> _____?

3rd para.   After the phone call, how did you feel? Why?

ACTIVITY C   Write a short composition about the following:

1. Do you like to receive phone calls? Why or why not?
2. If someone calls you and you don't want to talk to that person, what do you do?

The Test

ACTIVITY A   Ask your partner or someone in your group these questions. Then your partner or someone in your group will ask you the questions.

1. When did you last take a test?
2. What kind of test was it?
3. Did you study or practice for it?
4. How did you feel before the test?
5. How long was the test?
6. Was it easy or difficult?
7. Did you pass it?
8. Did most of the students pass or fail the test?
9. How did you feel after the test?
10. Did you speak to others who took the test? Did they like it? Why or why not?

ACTIVITY B   Write about a test that you took recently. Write three paragraphs.

1st para.

Did you take a test *yesterday?*
                    last week?
                    two weeks ago?
_____?

Was it *an English test?*
       a math test?
       a driving test?
       a _____?

Did you prepare for the test *for one hour?*
                             for three hours?
_____?

Did you feel *nervous before the test?*   *confident before the test?*

2nd para.

Was the test *45 minutes long?*
             one hour long?
             two hours long?
_____?

Was it *easy?   difficult?*
Did you *pass the test?   fail the test?*
Did you get *an A on the test?*
            a B on the test?
            75% on the test?
_____?

Did most of the students *pass the test?   fail the test?*
After the test did most of the students say that they *liked the test?*
                                                      didn't like the test? } Why?

3rd para.

After the test, did you feel *happy?*
                             sad?
                             depressed?
_____?

ACTIVITY C   Write a short composition about the following:

1. When you have to take a test, how do you feel?

2. How do you prepare for a test?

The First Day of English Class

ACTIVITY A   Ask your partner or someone in your group these questions. Then your partner or someone in your group will ask you the questions.

1. Why did you decide to take an English course?
2. How did you feel on the first day of class? Why?
3. What was your first impression of your teacher?
4. What did the teacher do to make you feel comfortable?
5. What did the teacher tell you to do?
6. Did you understand everything the teacher said? If not, why?
7. Did you meet any of your classmates the first day? Who?
8. At the end of the first class, how did you feel? Why?

ACTIVITY B   Write about the first day of your English course. Write four paragraphs.

1st para.

Did you decide to take
an English course *because you want to study in the United States?*
      because you want to have a good job?
      because you need English for your present job?
      because you plan to live in the United States?
      because you like the English language?

      because _____?

On the first day of class were you *excited? happy? nervous?*
      afraid? _____? } **Why?**

2nd para.

Did your teacher seem *friendly? helpful? strict?* _____?

Did your teacher try to make you feel comfortable and secure in the class?
How? *by smiling at you? by welcoming you to the class?*
    by speaking slowly? by explaining everything carefully?
    by _____?

3rd para.

Did your teacher tell you *to fill out a questionnaire?   to introduce yourself?*
         to buy books for the next class day?
         to do a homework assignment?
         to _____?

Did you understand everything the teacher said?
Yes? Why? *Because he/she spoke slowly?*
        Because he/she spoke in your native language?
        _____?

Why not? *because you were nervous?*
      because you didn't understand very much English?
      because the teacher spoke too fast?

      because _____?

4th para.

Did you meet any of your classmates the first day? Who?
At the end of your first class how did you feel?
    Did you want to come back to the next class?
    Did you want to drop the course? } **Why?**
    Did you have a stronger desire to learn English?

ACTIVITY C   Write a short composition about the following: What are the most important qualities of a teacher?

A Decision

ACTIVITY   With your partner, talk about Peter's decision to come to the United States. Using the choices you are given, you and your partner decide what you want to write. Then write three paragraphs. Each of you write on your own paper.

1st para.

Did Peter decide
to come to the United States *because he wanted to study?*
because he wanted to make money?
because life was too hard in his country?
_____?

Did Peter decide to come *after he finished high school?*
before he finished high school?
when he was _____ *years old?*
_____?

Did his parents feel *happy about his decision?   sad about his decision?* Why?

2nd para.

What year did he arrive in the United States?
When he first arrived, did he live *in Chicago?*
in San Francisco?
in New York?
in _____?

Did he live *with relatives?*
with a friend?
by himself?
_____?

Did he *get a job?   go to school?* Why?
Was he *happy?   homesick?*

3rd para.

Six months ago, did Peter *get sick?*
lose his job?
graduate from college?
meet someone special?
_____?

Did he decide *to get married?*
to go back to his native country?
to learn more English?
to find a job?
to _____?

Recycling

ACTIVITY   With your partner, talk about Marcia and her children. You and your partner decide what you want to write. You may use the choices given or write your own ideas. Write four paragraphs. Each of you write on your own paper.

1st para.

Did Marcia and her children decide to recycle waste?

Did they get information about recycling from the *newspaper?*
television?
government publications?
their friends?

_____?

2nd para.

Were they told to separate *old newspapers?*
plastic containers?
glass jars?

_____?

Did Marcia *wash out used jars?*
rinse out used plastic containers?
tie old newspapers into bundles?

_____?

Did her children *leave them outside their door?*
put them in special containers?
take them to the recycling center?

_____?

Did her children *return empty soda bottles to the store?*
take back empty soda cans?
collect empty cans and bottles in the street?

_____?

3rd para.

Did they talk to their neighbors about *recycling?*
protecting the environment?
ways they could help?

_____?

Did their neighbors *cooperate?   ignore them?   compliment them?*
tell them to go away?   agree to help?

_____?

Did they *call   write to   telephone   talk to* their government officials about establishing a recycling program in their community?

4th para.

Did they feel *good   happy   satisfied   frustrated* _____ about their efforts to improve the environment?

More About My Parents

ACTIVITY   Think about what your parents were like when you were a child. Use the following questions as a guide, and then add any information you would like to. Write three paragraphs.

1st para.

What is the first thing you remember about your mother?

What did your mother look like?

How tall was she?

How much did she weigh?

What color were her hair and eyes?

What kind of clothing did she wear?

What did your mother do for you when you were a child?

What were the most important things you learned from your mother?

2nd para.

What is the first thing you remember about your father?

What did your father look like?

How tall was he?

How much did he weigh?

What color were his hair and eyes?

What kind of clothing did he wear?

What did your father do for you when you were a child?

What were the most important things you learned from your father?

3rd para.

Did your father and mother have a good relationship? Explain.

How long did they live together?

Are they still alive?

If yes, where do they live now?

My Favorite Relative

ACTIVITY   Write about your favorite relative when you were a child. You may write about a sister, brother, aunt, uncle, cousin, grandmother, grandfather, etc., but *not* your mother or father. Write three paragraphs.

1st para.
  - Who was your favorite relative when you were a child?
  - What did he/she look like?
  - Where did he/she live?
  - How often did you see him/her?

2nd para.
  - What did you do together when you were a child?
  - Why was he/she your favorite relative?
  - How much did you love him/her?
  - Which qualities or characteristics did you like about this relative?

3rd para.
  - Where is your relative now?
  - Do you have the same kind of relationship with him/her now?
  - Why or why not?

An Important Person

ACTIVITY   Think about a person who is important to you. Who is this person? Why is this person important to you? Write three paragraphs.

1st para.

Who is this person?

What is the name of the person who is important to you?

Is this person a relative, friend, neighbor, teacher, counselor?

Where does this person live?

What does this person do?

Is there anything else you want to tell about this person?

2nd para.

Why is this person important to you?

Write about some, or all of the following:

What did this person do for you?

How did this person help to change your life?

What did you learn from this person?

What did you do for this person?

How do you feel about this person?

How does this person feel about you?

3rd para.

What do you want to do for this person?

Do you want to give something to this person?

What do you hope for the future?

Is there anything else you want to write about?

Next Weekend

ACTIVITY   Ask your partner these questions. Then your partner will ask you the questions. Write *your* answers about *yourself*.

1. What will you do Friday evening?
2. Who will you be with on Friday?
3. What will you do during the day on Saturday?
4. Will you go out Saturday night?
5. What will you do Sunday morning?
6. How will you spend the rest of the day on Sunday?
7. What will you do Sunday night?
8. Are you looking forward to the weekend? Why?

Now write a paragraph about what you will do next weekend. You may use the paragraph below as a model.

> Next weekend I will do many things. Friday evening I will have dinner with my family. After dinner we will play games and watch television. Saturday morning I will clean my home and take care of the laundry. Then I will buy food for the week. In the afternoon I will sit in the park and enjoy the fresh air. In the evening I will go out to dinner with someone. Then we will see a movie. Later that night we will go to a dance. I will sleep late on Sunday. When I get up I will prepare a nice brunch and read the paper. Then I will go out for some exercise. At night I will do my homework and get everything ready for the week. I am looking forward to the weekend because it is a time to catch up on work and also to relax and be with family and friends.

A Trip Together

ACTIVITY A   Ask a partner these questions. Then your partner will ask you the questions.

1. Will any of your friends or relatives take a trip soon? Who? When will they go?
2. Where will they go?
3. How will they go there?
4. Will they visit relatives or friends?
5. What will they do there?
6. Will they take pictures and send postcards?
7. Will they buy many things?
8. How will they feel when they get home?

ACTIVITY B   Write a story about the trip that George and Mary will take together. Write one paragraph.

1. Will George and Mary take a trip *next summer?*
                                    during the Christmas vacation?
                                    during the Easter vacation?
                    _____?

2. Will they go to *their native country?*
                    Florida?
                    Canada?
                    _____?

3. Will they *go by ship?*
                go by bus?
                drive?
                fly?
                    _____?

4. Will they *visit relatives?*
                visit friends?
                    _____?

5. Will they *take sightseeing tours every day?*
                play tennis every morning?
                lie on the beach all day?
                eat gourmet dinners every night?
                    _____?

6. Will they *take a lot of photographs?*
                make a videotape?
                send postcards to their friends?
                    _____?

7. Will they *shop for gifts?*
                buy clothing?
                buy souvenirs?
                    _____?

8. When George and Mary come home from their trip,
        will they be *rested?*
                    tired?
                    angry with each other?   ⎫
                    happy they spent time together? ⎬ Why?
                    _____?   ⎭

ACTIVITY C   Write a short composition about the following:
Is it more fun to travel with someone or to travel alone?

After Graduation

ACTIVITY   Hector is your friend. With a partner, talk about what Hector will do after he graduates. Using the choices you are given, you and your partner decide what you will write. Then write three paragraphs. Each of you write on your own paper.

1st para.

1. Will Hector graduate in *June?   January?*

2. When Hector graduates, *will he take a vacation?*
    look for a job?
    apply to another school?
    _____?

3. Will he have more time for *reading?   sports?   hobbies?   resting?*
    _____?

4. Will he move to another *home?   city?   country?*

2nd para.

5. Will he look for a job *with a high salary?*
    with good opportunities?
    that will pay for more education?
    that will give him good training?
    _____?

6. Will he *continue to go to school?*
    stop going to school?
    study at home?
    _____?

7. Will he attend classes at a *four-year school?   graduate school?*
    business school?   professional school?

3rd para.

8. Will he *get married?*
    have a child?
    have a new girlfriend?
    make new friends?
    _____?

9. Will he spend more time with his *wife?   children?   friends?*
    _____?

10. Will he be *happier?*
    more confident?
    wealthier?
    more satisfied with his life?
    _____ ?

40

My Future

ACTIVITY   Tell your partner or your group about your plans for the future. Then write about yourself. Write three paragraphs.

1st para.
> When this class or semester is over, what will you do?
>   Will you continue school? Where?
>   Will you get a degree? In what subject?
>   Will you go to another school? Where?

2nd para.
> Will you get a job? What kind?
> Will you travel? Where?
> Will you buy anything?   A car?   A house? _____?

3rd para.
> Will you help *your friends?*
>   *your parents?* } How?
>   *your children?*
> Will you help your community? How?
> Will you be satisfied with your life? Explain?

Happy Birthday

ACTIVITY A   Write about your birthday. Use the questions below as a guide. Write three paragraphs.

1st para. ⌈ Do you like birthdays? Why or why not?
⌊ How do you usually celebrate your birthday?

2nd para. ⌈ What did you do on your last birthday?
  Did you have a party?
  Did you have a special dinner?
  Did you celebrate with relatives and friends?
⌊ Did you get presents?

3rd para. ⌈ How will you celebrate your next birthday?
⌊ Is there anything that you didn't do last time that you will do next time?

ACTIVITY B   Write a short composition about the following: In general, are birthdays important? Why?

A Religious Holiday

ACTIVITY   Which religious holiday is the most important to you? Tell your partner or your group about how you celebrated that holiday when you were a child and how you celebrated (or will celebrate) this year. After you have shared this information, write about your holiday. You may use the following questions as a guide. Write five paragraphs.

1st para.
How did you celebrate this holiday when you were a child?

Did you have a party?

Did you go to religious services?

Did you have special meals?

What other customs or rituals did you follow?

2nd para.
How did you (will you) celebrate the holiday this year?

Did you (Will you) give a party?

Did you (Will you) go to religious services?

Did you (Will you) make a special meal?

What other customs or rituals did you (will you) follow?

3rd para.   Mention three things you didn't (won't) do.

4th para.   How was the holiday (How will the holiday be) different this year from the way you celebrated it as a child?

5th para.   Did you enjoy the holiday more in your native country, or do you enjoy it more now? Why?

A Letter

ACTIVITY   Write a letter to a friend or relative. The following questions can help you.

1. What are you doing right now?

2. What is the weather like?

3. Where are you going to school? What are you studying?

4. What else are you doing now?

5. What are you planning to do in the future?

    What courses are you planning to take?

    Where are you going during your next vacation?

6. What is your correspondent doing now? What are his/her plans?

Read the letter below. You may use it as a model if you want to.

888 Beach Avenue
Miami, Florida
October 15, 1994

Dear Ricardo,

　　I am sitting on a bench in my neighborhood park and enjoying the beautiful fall weather here. The wind is blowing, and some leaves are falling. I am going to college now and I am studying English. I am also working part-time as an elevator operator.

　　I am now sharing an apartment with my brother Tony and his wife Sara. He is working in a factory, and she is going to school. Together we are fixing up the apartment. Tony and Sara are planning to go back home for a visit at Christmas, but I am staying in the city to work.

　　Are you still going to school? What are you going to do at Christmas? Write to me soon.

Your friend,
Nelson

The Bank Robbery

ACTIVITY   Talk about the picture below with a partner. Together tell a story that explains what you see in the picture. Then write the story together by answering the following questions. Write one paragraph.

1. What are the four men doing?

2. What is the man in front doing with the gun?

3. What is he telling the cashier to do?

4. Why is she shaking?

5. Are the other tellers doing anything?

6. What is another robber doing to the guard?

7. What is the guard doing?

8. What is a third robber doing to the customers?

9. What is the fourth robber doing?

10. What are you going to do?

The Tube Boob

ACTIVITY   There are three people in the picture below: Ed; Ed's wife, Mabel (she's the one smiling and talking); and her friend, Maryanne. Discuss the picture with a partner. Together tell a story that explains what you see in the picture. Then write the story together by answering the following questions. Write three paragraphs on a separate piece of paper. Begin the story this way:

The Tube Boob

This   story   is   taking   place   in   a   _____.   There   are   many _____ standing   around   the   room. _____

1st para.
- Where is this story taking place?
- What things are standing all around the room?
- What things are lying on top of the television sets?
- Are the television sets working?
- What are Mabel and Maryanne doing?
- What is Ed doing?

2nd para.
- What is Ed smoking?
- Why is Mabel smiling?
- Why isn't Maryanne smiling?

3rd para.
- What is Mabel telling Maryanne?

Barroom Brawl

ACTIVITY   Discuss the picture above with a partner. Together, make up a story that explains what you see in the picture. Then write the story together by answering the following questions.

1. Where is this incident taking place?

2. What are the customers doing?

3. Are they saying anything?

4. Describe what each pair of customers is doing. You may use the following verbs: *lean, grab, threaten, fight, swing, try, lift, defend, hit, punch, fall, struggle, drop, lie, sit, strangle.*

   Example: One of the patrons *is leaning* back with his elbows on the bar. The man in front of him is _____. Behind them a man and woman *are fighting*. The woman is _____.

5. What are the bartenders doing?

6. Are they stopping the fight?

7. One is telling the other how the fight started. What is he saying?

How To

ACTIVITY

1. Think of a special skill that you have—something that you can do that most of the other students in the class probably do not know how to do. For example:

Prepare a Special Dish	Convert from Metric to	Play Checkers or Dominoes
Diaper a Baby	English Measure	Repair a Broken Window
Put Up Wallpaper	Score in Bowling	Fasten a Tie

2. Select a partner. Choose a skill that your partner does not know. Explain it to him/her. Answer his/her questions.
3. Reverse roles. As the learner, you should ask questions and take notes.
4. Write down the directions to the skill you are teaching. Give it a title: "How to . . ."
5. Write down the directions to the skill you have just learned about. Give it a title: "How to . . ."
6. Compare papers with your partner. Help each other make corrections.

Before you begin, read the recipe below. You may use it as a model.

How to Prepare Humus

Humus is a Middle Eastern appetizer dip popular in such countries as Greece, Turkey, Israel, and Lebanon. It is made from chickpeas and tehini (sesame seed paste). You need a food processor to make this dish.

Put the following ingredients in a food processor fitted with the metal chopping blade: 2 peeled garlic cloves; 2 one-pound cans of chickpeas (drained); 1 cup tehini; juice of one lemon; 1/3 cup water. Turn on the food processor, and puree the mixture for about two minutes or until it is smooth. Taste the humus, and add salt and pepper if needed. Blend for a few seconds. Empty the humus into a bowl, and chill in the refrigerator.

To serve, spread a thin layer in the center of a large plate, and cover with a little olive oil and paprika. Surround it with triangles of pita bread for dipping.

SECTION TWO

Filling In

Fire Fighters

ACTIVITY A   Read the following story. Then working as a group, choose two different words or short phrases for the blank spaces in each sentence. Any choice is correct if it makes sense in the story.

There are ten fire fighters in this (1) _____*picture*_____. They are fighting with each

(2) _____*drawing*_____.

other. They are not (1) _____ the fire.

(2) _____

Two men are (1) _____ the fight.

(2) _____

One is telling the other how it (1) _____.

(2) _____.

50

This is what he is saying:

"This house is located (1) _____ two different fire companies. These

(2) _____

companies don't like each other. They are (1) _____ competitive.

(2) _____

For example, they have an annual (1) _____ and always end up fighting.

(2) _____

They both (1) _____ to fight the same fire at the same time, and of course

(2) _____

they are fighting each other instead. I'm (1) _____ that it's not my house.

(2) _____

ACTIVITY B   Working by yourself, choose the word or short phrase in each sentence
that you like best in the story, "Fire Fighters." Underline your choice. Then recopy the story
with the words and phrases that you underlined.

Example

There are ten fire fighters in this (1) _____ *picture* _____.

(2) _____ *drawing* _____.

Recopy: *There are ten fire fighters in this picture. They are*

fighting with each other. . . .

Moneybags

ACTIVITY A   Read the following story. Then working as a group, choose two different words or short phrases for the blank spaces in each sentence. Any choice is correct if it makes sense in the story.

Mr. P. J. Gorman, the man (1) _____ *on the left* _____, is a very (1) _____ *rich* _____

(2) _____ *with the cigar* _____,   (2) _____ *wealthy* _____

man. You can tell by looking at him. He (1) _____ expensive cigars and

(2) _____

(1) _____ imported wine. He (1) _____ a big

(2) _____   (2) _____

house and he (1) _____ expensive clothing. He does one very

(2) _____

(1) _____ thing, however. He (1) _____ his money at

(2) _____   (2) _____

home in big bags. He likes to sit (1) _____ his money.

                                   (2) _____

His friend, Rocky Nelson, an ex- (1) _____ champion, is visiting him.

                                 (2) _____

Rocky is the owner of a (1) _____. Rocky (1) _____

                        (2) _____.   (2) _____

some money. He is (1) _____ P. J. about the money. What is he saying?

                   (2) _____

ACTIVITY B   Working by yourself, choose the word or short phrase in each sentence that you like best in the story, "Moneybags." Underline your choice. Then recopy the story with the words and phrases that you underlined.

Example

Mr. P. J. Gorman, the man (1) _____*on the left*_____, is a very

                          (2) _____*with the cigar*_____,

(1) _____*rich*_____ man.

(2) _____*wealthy*_____

Recopy: *Mr. P. J. Gorman, the man on the left, is a very wealthy*

man. You can tell by looking at him. He . . .

ACTIVITY C   Write down the words that Rocky is saying to P. J. Then write what P. J. says to Rocky.

The Time Machine

ACTIVITY A   Read the following story. Then working as a group, choose two different words or short phrases for the blank spaces in each sentence. Any choice is correct if it makes sense in the story.

"Crazy Doc" Johnson, head of the (1) _____ department at your school, says

(2) _____

he (1) _____ a time machine that can send people back in time. He wants

(2) _____

someone to test the machine, and he is offering (1) _____ to anyone who

(2) _____

will try it. You volunteer. Why? First of all, you (1) _____ what he is

(2) _____

offering. Secondly, "Crazy Doc" never invents anything that really (1) _____.

(2) _____.

So you (1) _____ that you have nothing to lose.

(2) _____

Doc Johnson (1) _____ you into his strange-looking machine and asks

(2) _____

you when and where back into time you would like to (1) _____. You tell

(2) _____.

him, and you laugh to yourself because you know it won't (1) _____.

(2) _____.

Doc (1) _____ a (1) _____ and the machine starts

(2) _____   (2) _____

shaking. You become afraid and you (1) _____. When the

(2) _____.

machine stops moving, you (1) _____. It has worked!

(2) _____.

You are back in the time and place that you (1) _____.

(2) _____.

ACTIVITY B   Working by yourself, choose the word or short phrase in each sentence that you like best in the story, "The Time Machine." Underline your choice. Then recopy the story with the words and phrases that you underlined.

ACTIVITY C   Write the conclusion of the story. Where does the machine take you? What year is it? Tell whom you meet and what you do.

Caught in the Act

ACTIVITY A   Read the following story. Then working as a group, choose three different words or short phrases for the blank spaces in each sentence. Any choice is correct if it makes sense in the story.

We entered and sat at a table near the (1) _____. The orchestra was just

(2) _____.

(3) _____.

(1) _____ to warm up. It was a/an (1) _____ evening and

(2) _____   (2) _____

(3) _____   (3) _____

the club was filled with (1) _____ who wanted to dance. They were waiting

(2) _____

(3) _____

impatiently for the (1) _____ to begin. Finally the orchestra started to play.

(2) _____

(3) _____

Their first number was (a) (1) _____. My lover and I

(2) _____.

(3) _____.

(1) _____ and walked to the dance floor. The music was

(2) _____

(3) _____

(1) _____. We danced the whole set without (1) _____.

(2) _____.   (2) _____.

(3) _____.   (3) _____.

When the orchestra took a break, my lover went (1) _____. When $\left\{ \begin{array}{l} he \\ she \end{array} \right\}$

(2) _____.

(3) _____.

returned to our table, ⎰ he ⎱ found me (1)_____ another ⎰ woman. ⎱
　　　　　　　　　　⎱ she ⎰　　　　　　　　　　　　　　　　⎱ man. ⎰

　　　　　　　　　　　　　(2)_____

　　　　　　　　　　　　　(3)_____

ACTIVITY B　　Working by yourself, choose the word or short phrase in each sentence that you like best in the story, "Caught in the Act." Underline your choice. Then recopy the story with the words and phrases that you underlined.

ACTIVITY C　　Working as a group, discuss different possible endings for the story. Then by yourself, choose the ending that you like best, and write your ending to the story.

A Bad Dream

ACTIVITY   Look at the picture and then read the story below. Parts of the story are missing. Discuss the story with your partner or your group. Then by yourself, fill in the missing parts of the story.

Frank is 45 years old. He is 5 feet, 6 inches tall and weighs about 190 pounds. He lives in a big city with his wife and two children.

Frank has an interesting job. He _____

_____

_____

Usually Frank stands with his cart _____

_____

_____

_____

One summer night Frank had no business at all. No one wanted to buy his sausages. He became so frustrated that he ate four of his own sausages with lots of mustard and onions. Then he went home and went directly to bed.

That night, Frank had a bad dream. He dreamed _____

_____

_____

_____

_____

_____

_____

_____

_____

_____.

Frank woke up in a sweat, which was strange because the air conditioner was on. His stomach was upset and he had a headache. He took an antacid and went back to bed.

In the future, Frank will not _____

_____

_____.

Gift Basket

ACTIVITY   Look at the picture and then read the story below. Three parts of the story are missing: what the note said, what Charley said, and what he decided to do. Discuss the story with your partner or your group. Then by yourself fill in the missing parts of the story.

Charley Moody was getting ready to go to bed. He was in his pajamas and was wearing his bathrobe. He was watching the 11 o'clock news. He heard the doorbell ring. When he opened the door, no one was there except a baby lying in a basket on the front step. There was a note pinned to the baby. The note said:

"_____

_____

_____

_____."

Charley read the note and then shouted, "_____

_____

_____

_____."

Charley decided _____

_____

_____.

Talking It Over

The Checkout Line

Mr. Becker is standing in the checkout line at a supermarket with a basketful of groceries. It is the end of the day. He is tired. He wants to get home as quickly as possible. He is next in line to be checked out. He doesn't want anyone to get in front of him.

Mrs. Dorsey came into the supermarket to buy milk and cookies for her child. She is in a hurry. There is a long line. She asks Mr. Becker if she can go ahead of him.

ACTIVITIES **Role Playing.** You and your partner decide who will be Mr. Becker and who will be Mrs. Dorsey. Say to each other the things that you think Mr. Becker and Mrs. Dorsey said to each other in the checkout line.

Dialogue Writing. When you and your partner finish the conversation, write it *all* down. Each of you write it on your own paper, like this:

Mrs. Dorsey: Excuse me sir. May I get ahead of you?

Mr. Becker: I'm sorry.

Mrs. Dorsey: _____

Mr. Becker: _____

Dialogue Correcting: When you and your partner finish writing, check each other's papers and correct any mistakes. Then read your dialogue out loud two times. One time you will be Mrs. Dorsey and the other time you will be Mr. Becker. Listen and correct any mistakes on your papers.

A Conversation in the Park

Carole is a young woman. She has two children but is divorced. She would like to meet someone and perhaps get married again. Yesterday Carole brought her children to the park. It was a beautiful spring day. Carole felt happy. She sat on a bench and watched her children play.

Richard is forty-seven years old. He lives alone. His wife died four years ago. His three children are married. He would like to meet a nice woman and perhaps get married again. Yesterday he went to the park during his lunch hour. He saw Carole sitting on a bench. He sat down next to her and began talking to her.

ACTIVITIES

Role Playing. You and your partner decide who will be Carole and who will be Richard. Say to each other the things you think Carole and Richard said to each other yesterday in the park.

Dialogue Writing. When you and your partner finish the conversation, write it *all* down. Each of you write it on your own paper, like this:

Richard: Hi. It's a beautiful day.

Carole: Yes. It's a nice day to be in the park.

Richard: _____

_____

Carole: _____

_____

Dialogue Correcting. When you and your partner finish writing, check each other's papers and correct any mistakes. Then read your dialogue out loud two times. One time you will be Carole and the other time you will be Richard. Listen and correct any mistakes on your papers.

63

I Won't Pay the Rent

Tenant There is no heat or hot water in your apartment. The toilet in your bathroom is not working properly. The super (janitor) doesn't clean the building or do anything else he is supposed to do. He sits on the front steps drinking and talking to his friends. The building is full of roaches, the halls are dirty, and you are angry. You complain to the landlord. You tell him you won't pay the rent until everything is fixed and he gets a new janitor (super) for the building.

Landlord This building has an old boiler and it is broken. You called the repair service and they say it will take another week to fix it. You would like to get a new super (janitor), but they're hard to find. If the building is dirty and has roaches, it's because of the dirty tenants. You're not making enough profit on the building to maintain it properly. You want your rent right now.

ACTIVITIES   **Role Playing.**   You and your partner decide who will be the tenant and who will be the landlord. Say to each other the things you think the tenant and the landlord would say to each other.

Dialogue Writing.   When you and your partner finish the conversation, write it *all* down. Each of you write it on your own paper, like this:

Tenant: _____

Landlord: _____

Dialogue Correcting.   When you and your partner finish writing, check each other's papers and correct any mistakes. Then read your dialogue out loud two times. One time you will be the tenant and the other time you will be the landlord. Listen and correct any mistakes on your papers.

Home for the Holiday?

Jenny has lived in Boston for three years. Her parents still live in their native country. They want Jenny to come home for the holiday vacation.

Their reasons
{
She is their oldest child and they haven't seen her in two years.
Their other children are not at home.
They don't want to celebrate the holiday alone.
Jenny's mother is not feeling well.
}

Jenny does not want to go home for the holiday.

Her reasons
{
Her friends invited her to spend part of the holiday vacation with them.
She has a boyfriend and she wants to be with him.
She is going to school and she has a lot of work to do during the vacation.
It costs a lot of money to fly home and back.
Jenny is afraid her parents will ask her to stay with them and not return to Boston.
}

A week before the holiday, Jenny calls her parents on the phone to discuss the situation with them.

ACTIVITIES   **Role Playing.**   You and your partner decide who will be Jenny and who will be the mother (or father). Say to each other the things you think Jenny and her mother (or father) said to each other when she called on the phone.

Dialogue Writing.   When you and your partner finish the conversation, write it *all* down. Each of you write it on your own paper, like this:

Jenny: _____

                            _____

Mother (or Father): _____

                            _____

Dialogue Correcting.   When you and your partner finish writing, check each other's papers and correct any mistakes. Then read your dialogue out loud two times. One time you will be Jenny and the other time the mother (or father). Listen and correct any mistakes on your papers.

Final Grade

Student   Your English teacher gave you a final grade of C. You think you deserve a better grade. Your attendance was good. You passed all your tests and you did most of your homework. Besides, your friend got a higher grade and you know more English than him/her. You go to your teacher and ask for a better grade.

Teacher   You decide on final grades carefully. They are based on

1. the final examination (which includes a composition marked by other teachers).
2. all work done during the course.
3. how much progress the student made during the course.

This student did all the work and got a passing grade on the final exam but didn't make much progress during the course. You do not want to raise the grade.

ACTIVITIES   **Role Playing.**   You and your partner decide who will be the student and who will be the teacher. Say to each other the things you think the student and the teacher said to each other.

Dialogue Writing.   When you and your partner finish the conversation, write it *all* down. Each of you write it on your own paper, like this:

Student: _____

_____

Teacher: _____

_____

Dialogue Correcting.   When you and your partner finish writing, check each other's papers and correct any mistakes. Then read your dialogue out loud two times. One time you will be the student and the other time you will be the teacher. Listen and correct any mistakes on your papers.

A Mother–Daughter Conflict

Mrs. Martinez came to the United States as an adult. She has three children and is raising them according to the customs of her native country. She is very strict with her children, especially her teenage daughters. She doesn't permit her daughters to stay outside after school. She doesn't permit them to go out with boys or go to parties with friends. Mrs. Martinez loves her children and believes that she is raising them the best way.

Maria is her seventeen-year-old daughter. She was born in this country. She is now a junior in high school. Maria's friends in school have more freedom than she has. She feels unhappy because she would like to spend time with them having fun. However, her mother makes her go right home after school.

Recently, a classmate named Louis told her that he likes her and would like to go out with her. Maria feels attracted to him and would like to accept his invitation.

Last night after her brother and sister had gone to bed, Maria talked to her mother about her desire to go out with Louis.

ACTIVITIES   **Role Playing.**   You and your partner decide who will be Maria and who will be Mrs. Martinez (male students can be Maria's older brother Tony if they wish). Say to each other the things you think Maria and her mother (or brother) said to each other.

Dialogue Writing.   When you and your partner finish the conversation, write it *all* down. Each of you write it on your own paper, like this:

Maria: _____

_____

Mother (or Brother):   _____

_____

Dialogue Correcting.   When you and your partner finish writing, check each other's papers and correct any mistakes.

Reading.   Read the following story about the decision that Maria made after talking to her mother.

Maria's Decision

Maria talked with her mother last night after her brother and sister were sleeping. She told her mother about Louis. She asked her mother if she could go to the movies with him. Mrs. Martinez got very upset. She yelled at Maria and told her that she couldn't have a boyfriend until she finished high school. She told her not to see or talk to Louis again. Maria felt very bad. She went to her room and cried. After a while she stopped crying and started thinking. She said to herself, "I am 17 years old. I am old enough to have a boyfriend. I am not going to obey my mother. I am going to see Louis tomorrow in school and we are going to make plans to go to the movies."

Writing.   You and your partner complete this story.

Telling Stories

Picture Story 1

ACTIVITY   Discuss this picture with a partner. Together make up a story that explains what you see in the picture. Then write the story this way:

1. Explain what is happening right now in this picture. Describe the room. Tell where each person is and what he or she is doing. Tell how each person is reacting to the face in the window.

2. Tell a story about these people. Who are they? Why is the man standing at the window? How does the story end? What will happen?

Write this story *by yourself*. Then correct it *together*. Write a title for the story.

Picture Story 2

ACTIVITY   Discuss this photograph with your partner or your group. Together, make up a story that explains what you see in the photograph. Then, write the story yourself. Correct it together with a partner. Write a title for the story.

Picture Story 3

ACTIVITY   Talk about this photograph with your partner or your group. Together, make up a story that explains the photograph. Who are the two people? Where are they? Why are they smiling?

Then, write the story yourself.

After you have finished, correct it together with a partner.

Write a title for the story.

Picture Story 4

ACTIVITY   Discuss this picture with your partner. Together, make up a story that explains the picture.

Then write this story *by yourself*. When you have finished, correct it with your partner. Write a title for the story.

Picture Story 5

ACTIVITY   Imagine that you are sitting outside. You are alone; no one else is near you. There isn't any noise. The day is very beautiful.

Daydream for ten minutes. Then write some of your daydream.

Picture Story 6

ACTIVITY   Discuss this photograph with a partner. Together make up a story that explains what you see in the photograph.

Then write the story *by yourself*. When you have finished, correct it with a partner. Write a title for the story.

Putting an End to It

Julia's Story

Julia was eighteen years old and she was finishing high school. She wanted to be a professional, but there were few opportunities in her country. First, it was difficult to go to school because it was expensive, and priority was given to men. Second, even if she could go to school, there were very few jobs available. Finally, her parents did not approve and would not help her.

Julia had an older brother who lived in New York. He said she could come to live with him and go to school at the same time. There were disadvantages to going to New York. She had a boyfriend, and he didn't want her to go. She knew that New York was dangerous and dirty and cold in the winter. She knew she would have to learn English and that it would be difficult for her.

Julia thought about going to New York, and she considered the advantages and disadvantages.

ACTIVITY   This is the beginning of a story. How would you finish this story? Discuss this with your partner or group. Then finish the story by yourself: What did Julia decide to do? Tell why. Also tell what happened to her.

If she decided to go to New York:
How did she explain her decision to her parents and boyfriend?
What happened to her after she came to New York?

If she decided to stay in her country:
What did she do about her ambitions to get an education and become a professional? Did she have to give them up, or was she able to work out a plan?

Was Julia happy or unhappy with her decision? Explain why.

The Note in the Bottle

I was walking along the beach one evening with my friend John. There was a full moon and the rippling waves glittered white in the moonlight. Suddenly we saw an object bobbing up and down in the waves. It was a bottle, and we could see that there was something inside it.

I walked out into the water and grabbed the bottle just as a big wave came in. I stumbled out of the water soaking wet and laughing. "I hope there's something interesting in this bottle," I said. There was. Inside the bottle we found a note and an old gold coin.

We read the note. It said:

ACTIVITY   Discuss this story with your partner or your group. Then write the ending of the story by yourself. Write the exact words in the note, and then tell what you and John did.

Love Letter

Marcia and John are in love. They want to get married, but they have some problems. Marcia wants to finish school and start her career before she has the responsibility of a family. She will not be ready to get married for at least two years. John's mother lives in his native country. His mother is seriously ill. John must go back to take care of her. He will not be back for six months.

After he leaves, John and Marcia write to each other. They write about their love for each other, and they suggest solutions to their problems.

ACTIVITY   Write the letter that Marcia sent to John or that John sent to Marcia.

Robert

Robert came to the United States with his parents and his younger sister when he was twelve. They lived in New York, and Robert went to school there. His father died when Robert was fourteen. After his father's death, Robert became much closer to his mother. He took care of her and protected her.

His mother remarried when he was sixteen. He tried very hard to like his stepfather, but his stepfather wouldn't accept him. Maybe he was jealous of the close relationship between Robert and his mother. The stepfather treated Robert very badly. Robert was in high school, and he didn't have any money. Day by day it was becoming more difficult for him to live in the same house with his stepfather. It was hard for Robert to talk to his mother about his feelings because he knew that she loved her new husband.

ACTIVITY   This is the beginning of a story. How would you finish this story? Discuss this with your partner or group. Then finish the story *by yourself*:

What decision did Robert make?
How did Robert's mother react to his decision?
What, if anything, changed between Robert and his mother?
What, if anything, changed between Robert and his stepfather?

Surprise Package

It was Saturday, June 13, a beautiful sunny day. I remember it well because that day my life changed—and it will never be the same again.

Here's what happened. I was just finishing my breakfast when the doorbell rang. It was a messenger with a package for me. I signed for it, brought it inside, and put it down on the hall table. I didn't have any idea what it was, or who had sent it. It was very puzzling.

I quickly took off the wrapping paper, and underneath there was a box with a ribbon around it. I untied the ribbon and opened the box.

ACTIVITY   Discuss the story with your partner or your group. Then write the ending of the story yourself. Tell what you found in the box and how it changed your life.

SECTION SIX

Exercising

My Brother

ACTIVITY   Read the story below and fill in the blanks with the *simple present* form of each verb. Where you see _____ write the negative form of the verb.
(neg.)

My brother _____ school. He _____ very hard. He
        like   study

_____ to mind. He also _____. My brother and I
   seem (neg.)   work

_____ a lot of time together. We _____ along very well.
    spend   get

We _____.
  fight (neg.)

My Classmate

ACTIVITY   Read the story below and fill in the blanks with the *simple present* form of each verb. Where you see _____ write the negative form of the verb.
(neg.)

My classmate's name _____ Elizabeth. She _____
         be   come

from Greece. She _____ 22 years old. She _____ in
       be   live

Westwood with her mother, father, and three sisters. Elizabeth _____
                     be (neg.)

married. She _____ any children, but she _____ to
    have (neg.)   hope

have a son and a daughter in the future. She is studying English because she

_____ to be a bilingual secretary. She also _____ that
   want   think

English _____ a beautiful language. In her free time, Elizabeth
     be

_____ tennis, _____ good books, and
   play   read

_____ out with her boyfriend. I _____ happy that
   go   be

Elizabeth _____ my classmate.
      be

My Dream House

ACTIVITY   Read the story below and fill in the blanks with the *simple present* form of each verb. Where you see _____ write the negative form of the verb.
(neg.)

I _____ in an apartment in a big city. The city
        live

_____ beautiful. I often _____ about having my own
        be   dream

house in the country. When I _____, I _____ a red
                                    dream   see

house with many tall trees. There _____ any other houses near it. Inside
                                        be (neg.)

the house there _____ a big living room with a fireplace. On one side of the
                        be

living room there _____ a big window. From the window you can
                        be

_____ a clear blue lake with a mountain behind it. Next to the living room
        see

_____ a small kitchen and upstairs _____ two
        be   be

bedrooms and a bathroom.

It _____ very hot during the summer. I _____
        be   think

about the cool water of the lake and the shade of the trees near my dream house. In winter,

when it _____ cold, I _____ that I
            be   imagine

_____ in my living room in front of a warm fire in the fireplace. Outside,
        be

the snow _____ and the wind _____, but I
                fall   blow

_____ it. I _____ nice and warm.
    mind (neg.)   be

86

A Married Couple

ACTIVITY A   Read the story below and fill in the blanks with the *simple present* form of each verb. Where you see _____ write the negative form of the verb.
(neg.)

John and Carole _____ married. They _____ each
be   love
other very much. They _____ to have children, but they
want
_____ any yet. They both _____. John
have (neg.)   work
_____ an auto mechanic, and Carole _____ a dental
be   be
technician. They _____ good salaries. They _____
make   spend
every evening together except Monday and Thursday. On Mondays, Carole

_____ classes at the college, and John _____ home and
take   stay
_____ Monday night football or _____ a book. On
watch   read
Thursdays, John _____ out bowling with friends, and Carole usually
go
_____ to a movie with a friend of hers. They _____ it's
go   think
important to have some time away from each other.

ACTIVITY B   Below are *questions* and *answers* about the story, "A Married Couple." On each line at the left, finish the question that goes with the answer.

Questions

1. Are _____ ?
2. Do _____ ?
3. Do _____ ?
4. Do _____ ?
5. What _____ ?
6. What _____ ?
7. When _____ ?
8. When _____ ?
9. What _____ ?
10. Why _____ ?

Answers

Yes, they are.

Yes, they do.

No, not yet.

Yes, they both work.

He is an auto mechanic.

She is a dental assistant.

Every evening except Monday and Thursday.

On Mondays.

John goes bowling, and Carole goes to a movie.

Because they think it's important to have time away from each other.

Allen

ACTIVITY A   Read the story below and fill in the blanks with the *simple present* form of each verb. Where you see _____ write the negative form of the verb.
(neg.)

I _____ a good friend named Allen. He _____ forty
      have   be

years old. He _____ 5 feet, 8 inches tall and _____
                          be   weigh

about 150 pounds. He _____ short, dark brown hair and
                                have

_____ eyeglasses. He _____ an attractive-looking man.
        wear   be

Allen _____ from Connecticut and _____ in New
              come   live

York City now. He used to live in Connecticut with his wife and two children, but he

_____ divorced and his two children _____ to college.
        be   go

Now Allen _____ alone in his own apartment in Manhattan.
                    live

Allen _____ four sisters and one brother. They
              have

_____ all married and _____ near New York. His
        be   live

mother _____ dead and his father _____ in a nursing
                  be   be

home.

Allen _____ a lawyer. He _____ his work and
              be   like

_____ a lot of money. He _____ a very generous and
        make   be

happy person.

ACTIVITY B   Below are *questions* and *answers* about the story, "Allen." On each line at the left, finish the question that goes with the answer.

Questions	Answers
1. *How old* _____?	Forty.
2. *How tall* _____?	5'8".
3. *How much* _____?	150 pounds.
4. *What* _____?	Dark brown.
5. *Where* _____?	Connecticut.
6. *Is* _____?	No, he is divorced.
7. *Does* _____?	Yes, he has two children.
8. *How many* _____?	Four.
9. *What* _____?	He is a lawyer.
10. *Is* _____?	Yes, he is.

Jose's New York

ACTIVITY   Read the story below and fill in the blanks with the *simple present* form of each verb. Where you see _____ write the negative form of the verb.
   (neg.)

Jose _____ New York. He frequently _____ up and
              like   walk
down Broadway and _____ at the people. He often
                                  look
_____ to watch the things that _____ on. Vendors
        stop   go
_____ fruits and vegetables. People _____ where they
        sell   look (neg.)
_____ and often _____ into others. There
        walk   bump
_____ much concern for other people. But there _____
     be (neg.)   be
good things too. Some people _____ and _____ "hello."
                                          stop   say
Someone may _____ on a little show. It _____ what
                      put   matter (neg.)
_____. It _____ a lot of fun.
     happen   be

The Class

ACTIVITY   Read the story below and fill in the blanks with the *simple present* form of each verb. Where you see _____ write the negative form of the verb.
   (neg.)

John _____ in class. William _____. Freddy and
              be   be (neg.)
Charlie _____ here, but they _____ to work. Sarah
                be   want (neg.)
_____ like she _____ to go home. Allen
        look   want
_____ to do his homework. Sam _____ the work.
     like (neg.)   understand (neg.)
Some students _____ too much, but most of them
                          talk
_____ anything. Harry _____ what to do. Barbara
     say (neg.)   know (neg.)
_____ all the time. Philip _____ to work, but Dulce
        cry   try
_____ bothering him. It _____ 12 o'clock. The class
        keep   be
_____ over. Thank God!
        be

Richard's Problem

ACTIVITY A Read the story below and fill in the blanks with the *simple present* form of each verb. Where you see _____ write the negative form of the verb.
(neg.)

Richard _____ some advice. He _____ in a big city
            need   live

with his wife and two children. He _____ to move to a better
                                          want

neighborhood, but he _____ if he should move at this time. In the first
                          know (neg.)

place, he _____ in a store near his home. He _____ to
              work   walk

his job every day. If he _____, he will have to spend money traveling to
                              move

work. Second, his two children _____ the school they are attending now.
                                        like

They _____ many friends in school. Maybe they won't like to go to a
          have

different school in a different neighborhood. In the third place, Richard

_____ a very good salary at his job. He _____ enough
     make (neg.)   earn

to support his family now, but he _____ sure he can support his wife and
                                        be (neg.)

children in a new apartment where the rent is a lot higher. Richard and his wife often

_____ about their situation. They _____ to move, but
     talk   prefer

they can't decide because they _____ the problems they will have if they
                                      realize

move.

ACTIVITY B Below are *answers* about the story, "Richard's Problem." On each line at the left, write a *question* that goes with the answer.

Questions   **Answers**

1. _____? Some advice.

2. _____? In a big city.

3. _____? To move to a better
                                                    neighborhood.

4. _____? In a store near his home.

5. _____? He walks.

6. _____? Yes, they do.

7. _____? Because they have many
                                                    friends.

8. _____? He isn't sure.

9. _____? Yes, they do.

10. _____? They will have problems
                                                    if they move.

Charlie's Grocery

ACTIVITY A   Read the story below and fill in the blanks with the *simple present* form of each verb. Where you see _____ write the negative form of the verb.
(neg.)

Charlie _____ a small grocery. He _____ a nice
    own   be

guy. All the people in the neighborhood _____ he _____
                                              know   be

a nice guy. Charlie's store _____ a little of everything. It
                                 have

_____ all kinds of groceries. For the kids there _____
    carry   be

snacks and sodas. In the back there _____ a shelf of school supplies.
                                         be

Behind the counter Charlie _____ cigarettes. People
                               keep

_____ in and out all day long. Sometimes one person
    run

_____ in five or six times a day. Charlie _____ all the
    come   mind (neg.)

business. Charlie _____ his store until 7 A.M., but most customers
                      open (neg.)

_____ in before 7:30. The kids _____ arriving at 8
    come (neg.)   start

o'clock. When they _____ for school it _____ quiet for
                       leave   be

a while. Then the women _____ to come in. Some of them just
                            begin

_____ to talk. Others _____ a few things and leave.
    want   buy

ACTIVITY B   Below are *answers* about the story. On each line at the left, write a *question* that goes with the answer.

Questions   **Answers**

1. _____ ? Charlie.

2. _____ ? Yes, he is.

3. _____ ? All the people.

4. _____ ? A little of everything.

5. _____ ? All kinds of groceries.

6. _____ ? Yes, there are.

7. _____ ? Yes, there is.

8. _____ ? Cigarettes.

9. _____ ? No, he doesn't.

10. _____ ? At 8 o'clock.

School Days

ACTIVITY   Read the story below and fill in the blanks with the *past tense* form of each verb. Where you see _____ (neg.) write the negative form of the verb.

When I _____ young, I always _____ to attend
        be   want

school, but I _____ old enough. I _____ my older sister
          be (neg.)   watch

go to school every day, and I _____ more and more jealous. Finally the day
                              get

_____. I _____ early in the morning and
    come   wake up

_____ my best dress. I _____ so excited I
   put on   be

_____ to eat breakfast. Then my mother _____ me to
   want (neg.)   take

school. A lot of strange children _____ there. They
                                       be

_____ to me. The teacher _____. I
   talk (neg.)   smile (neg.)

_____ asleep at my desk. When I _____ home, I
    fall   return

_____. I _____ that I _____ school.
    cry   decide   like (neg.)

My Parents

ACTIVITY   Read the story below and fill in the blanks with the *past tense* form of each verb. Where you see _____ (neg.) write the negative form of the verb.

My mother _____ born in San Juan, Puerto Rico in 1944. My father
              be

_____ born in Ponce, in 1932. My mother _____ to a
   be   go

public elementary school and then to Colegio San Juan. She _____ high
                                                              finish

school. My father _____ to school in Ponce until the eighth grade. He
                       go

_____ school because he _____ to help take care of his
 finish (neg.)   have

mother. My mother _____ two brothers and two sisters. She
                        have

_____ with her parents. My father _____ any sisters or
   live   have (neg.)

brothers. He _____ with his parents very long because his father
               live (neg.)

_____ and his mother _____ sick. He
    die   get

_____ with an uncle and _____ in his uncle's store so
   stay   work

that he _____ help support his mother.
            can

92

Gift Basket

ACTIVITY   Look at the picture on p. 60. Read the story below. Fill in the blanks with the *past tense* form of each verb. Where you see _____ write the negative form of the verb.
(neg.)

Charley Moody _____ ready to go to bed. He
get

_____ in his pajamas and he _____ on his bathrobe. He
be   have

_____ the 11 o'clock news. Then he _____ the doorbell
watch   hear

ring. When he _____ the door, he _____ what he
open   like (neg.)

_____. He _____ a baby lying in a basket on his front
see   find

step. There _____ a note pinned to the baby. It _____
be   be

from the mother and _____ why she _____ take care of
tell   can (neg.)

her baby. She _____ Mr. Moody to take care of the baby until she
ask

_____ do it herself. When he _____ the note, he
can   read

_____ angry and _____. He _____
get   shout   hope

the mother _____ hear him. He _____ that she
will   say

_____ irresponsible. He _____ to give her money to
be   offer

care for her baby. But she _____ back. Charley _____
come (neg.)   want

to call the police, but he _____ at the cute, smiling baby and
look

_____ to care for it until the mother _____.
decide   return

A Dinner Guest

ACTIVITY A   Read the story below and fill in the blanks with the **past tense** form of each verb. Where you see _____ (neg.) write the negative form of the verb.

Last night John and Mary _____ a friend to dinner. They
invite

_____ roast leg of lamb. They _____ a good Spanish
have   serve

wine. It _____ $10. Their guest _____ any because she
cost   drink (neg.)

_____ on a diet. She _____ a potato but she
be   eat

_____ any butter on it. The guest _____ some flowers.
put (neg.)   bring

After dinner they _____ for a while. Then they _____
talk   watch

television. They _____ up late because they _____ too
stay (neg.)   be

tired. They _____ their guest home at 10:30. It _____
send   be

cold and she _____ home by cab. Then John and Mary
get

_____ to bed.
go

ACTIVITY B   Below are *answers* about the story, "A Dinner Guest." On each line at the left, write a *question* that goes with the answer.

Questions		Answers
1. _____ ?		Last night.
2. _____ ?		Roast leg of lamb.
3. _____ ?		$10.
4. _____ ?		No, she didn't.
5. _____ ?		She was on a diet.
6. _____ ?		Yes, she did.
7. _____ ?		Some flowers.
8. _____ ?		No, they didn't.
9. _____ ?		At 10:30.
10. _____ ?		By cab.

Mexico City

ACTIVITY A   Read the story below, and fill in the blanks with the *past tense* form of each verb. Where you see _____, write the negative form of the verb.
(neg)

John _____ Mexico City. He frequently _____
like   walk

up and down the avenues and _____ at the people. He also
look

_____ to what they said. Although he _____ Spanish
listen   speak (neg)

and he _____ everything, he _____ enough to get along.
understand (neg)   know

He often _____ to look in shop windows. He _____
stop   have

trouble buying things but it _____ difficult for him to order meals in
be (neg.)

restaurants. He _____ enough Spanish for that. The best thing
speak

of all _____ that he _____ sick. Everyone
be   get (neg.)

else _____. He _____ that Mexican food
do   decide

_____ with him.
agree

ACTIVITY B   Below are *questions* and *answers* about the story, "Mexico City." On each line at the left, finish the *question* that goes with the answer.

Questions		Answers
1. *Who* _____ ?		John.
2. *Where* _____ ?		Up and down the avenues.
3. *Who(m)* _____ ?		The people.
4. *Did* _____ ?		No, he didn't.
5. *Why* _____ ?		To look in shop windows.
6. *Was* _____ ?		No, it wasn't.
7. *Did* _____ ?		No, he didn't.
8. *Who* _____ ?		Everyone else.
9. *What* _____ ?		That Mexican food agreed with him.

Fong Chi's Experience

ACTIVITY A   Read the story below and fill in the blanks with the *past tense* form of each verb. Where you see _____ write the negative form of the verb.
                                                   (neg.)

Fong Chi _____ born in Hong Kong. He _____ to
              be   decide

come to San Francisco four years ago to find a better life. When he _____
                                                                          arrive

at the airport, he _____ any money. He _____ to live
                      have (neg.)   go

with his uncle. His uncle _____ rich. He _____ Fong
                              be (neg.)   tell

Chi that he _____ to look for a job. Fong Chi _____
                  have   try

hard to find a job, but it _____ very difficult because he
                              be

_____ English. Finally he _____ a job in a factory in
    speak (neg.)   find

Chinatown. There _____ many other workers in the factory besides Fong
                      be

Chi. None of them _____ English either. After a few weeks, Fong Chi
                      speak

_____ the factory. He _____ all the hard work and the
    leave   like (neg.)

low pay. His uncle and his other relatives _____ happy about that. They
                                              be (neg.)

_____ the money that he _____ to help pay the
    need   earn

household expenses. Fong Chi _____ the situation. Soon he
                                  realize

_____ another job.
    find

96

ACTIVITY B   Below are *answers* about the story, "Fong Chi's Experience." On each line at the left, write a *question* that goes with the answer.

Questions   **Answers**

1. _____ ?   In Hong Kong.

2. _____ ?   To find a better life.

3. _____ ?   Four years ago.

4. _____ ?   No, he didn't.

5. _____ ?   His uncle.

6. _____ ?   No, he wasn't.

7. _____ ?   Because he didn't speak English.

8. _____ ?   He didn't like the hard work and the low pay.

9. _____ ?   No, they weren't.

10. _____ ?   Yes, he did.

My Uncle Carmine

ACTIVITY A   Read the story below and fill in the blanks with the *past tense* form of each verb. Where you see _____ (neg.) write the negative form of the verb.

My Uncle Carmine _____ to come to my house every weekend. He
                         use

_____ to hunt. He _____ in a big city, and we
     love   live

_____ a house in the country. Since he _____ hunt in
     have   can (neg.)

the city, he _____ to visit us. He always _____ carrying
                   come   arrive

two loaves of Italian bread. I _____ that bread but I never
                                     like

_____ enough of it. He _____ really my uncle but just
     get   be (neg.)

an old friend of the family. But he _____ a very good friend. He
                                          be

_____ me hunting with him every weekend. We _____
     take   walk

through the woods and _____ rabbits. One weekend we
                              hunt

_____ six. One winter I _____ out without my jacket
     shoot   go

and _____ a cold. I _____ to stay in bed but my parents
         catch   want (neg.)

_____ me. I _____ a terrible time. But usually I
     make   have

_____ OK, and when it _____ cold I
     be   be

_____. When we _____ hungry, we
     mind (neg.)   feel

_____ and _____ a fire. Uncle Carmine
     stop   build

_____ sausage over the fire, and we _____ it with big
     cook   eat

chunks of his bread. We _____ such a good time that we
                                have

_____ to leave.
     want (neg.)

98

ACTIVITY B   Below are *answers* about the story, "My Uncle Carmine." On each line at the left, write a *question* that goes with the answer.

Questions   **Answers**

1. _____ ?   Every weekend.

2. _____ ?   Hunt.

3. _____ ?   Because he couldn't
                                                      hunt in the city.

4. _____ ?   Italian bread.

5. _____ ?   No, he wasn't.

6. _____ ?   Yes, he was.

7. _____ ?   Rabbits.

8. _____ ?   Six.

9. _____ ?   Sausage and bread.

10. _____ ?   No, they didn't.

Tomorrow

ACTIVITY   Read the story below and fill in the blanks with the *future tense* form of each verb. Where you see _____ write the negative form of the verb.
(neg.)

Tomorrow morning I _____ to the city. I _____ for
return   _drive_

two hours. I _____ on the way. I _____ gas if I need it.
stop (neg.)   _get_

I _____ home about noon. I _____ lunch and then I
arrive   _have_

_____ some phone calls. I _____ time to relax. I
make   _have (neg.)_

_____ down and _____ to write a report. I
sit   _start_

_____ it by tomorrow night because it is due the next day. It
finish

_____ about twenty pages long. When I am finished, I
_be_

_____ dinner and _____ it easy. I
eat   _take_

_____ TV and I _____ out. Then I
watch (neg.)   _go (neg.)_

_____ just _____ down and _____
                  lie   _go_

to sleep.

Going to College

ACTIVITY   Read the story below and fill in the blanks with the *future tense* form of each verb. Where you see _____ write the negative form of the verb.
(neg.)

Next year I _____ to college. I _____ English and
_go_   _study_

_____ courses in math and science. I _____ for fifteen
take   _register_

credits. It _____ easy, but I _____ hard and if I need
be (neg.)   _work_

help, I _____ my teachers and my counselor. I _____
ask

also _____ a tutor. To pay for college, I _____ tuition
get   _request_

assistance. I _____ also _____ for a bank loan. To
                          apply

cover my personal expenses, I _____ for a part time job. It
                              look

_____ easy, but it _____ worth it. Some day I
be (neg.)   _be_

_____ with a diploma and _____ a good job and a
graduate   _have_

better life.

An Environmental Disaster?

ACTIVITY A   Read the story below and fill in the blanks with the *future tense* form of each verb. Where you see _____ write the negative form of the verb.
                                              (neg.)

Pessimists predict that the world _____ by the year 2050. This
                                                    end

_____ because companies _____ manufactured
          happen   release

chemicals into the air and cattle raisers _____ gradually

_____ large forests to make room for cattle grazing. Because of this, they
          destroy

say the ozone layer in the atmosphere that protects the earth from the sun's harmful rays

_____ depleted. As a result, people _____ of cancer,
          be   die

crops _____, and melting polar ice _____ terrible
         grow (neg.)   cause

flooding.

Optimists say this _____. People all over the world
                              happen (neg.)

_____ a change. Governments _____ laws forbidding
          demand   make

the manufacture and use of harmful chemicals. People _____ less meat so
                                                                 eat

that we _____ to raise more cattle. Governments _____
              need (neg.)   pass

laws protecting the forests because they _____ to risk total destruction.
                                                     want (neg.)

The earth _____ alive and well in the year 2050.
                    be

ACTIVITY B   Below are *answers* about the story, "An Environmental Disaster?" On each line at the left, write a question that goes with the answer.

Questions	Answers
1. _____?	In the year 2050.
2. _____?	Because of the release of manufactured chemicals.
3. _____?	Cattle raisers.
4. _____?	The ozone layer.
5. _____?	Melting polar ice.
6. _____?	People all over the world.
7. _____?	Make laws forbidding the manufacture and use of harmful chemicals.
8. _____?	Eat less meat.
9. _____?	Pass laws protecting the forests.
10. _____?	Because they will not want to risk total destruction.

101

Pete's Day

ACTIVITY A   Read the story below. Fill in the blanks with the *future tense* form of each verb. Where you see _____ write the negative form of the verb.
                                     (neg.)

Pete _____ time to see his girlfriend tomorrow. He
                have (neg.)

_____ busy all day and all night. In the morning he
        be

_____ his mother. She is an old woman and can't get around much
        visit

anymore so Pete _____ the shopping for her. He _____
                                do

also _____ her dog to the veterinarian. When he finishes that, he
            take

_____ his car to the garage. There is something wrong with the
        drive

transmission. He _____ for the car to be fixed. He
                        wait (neg.)

_____ later in the afternoon. He _____ to see a friend
        come back   go

who owes him some money. Then he _____ the train uptown to the office
                                        take

of his lawyer. He _____ to his lawyer about some legal matters concerning
                        talk

some property he owns in New Jersey. The lawyer _____ him some legal
                                                    give

papers to sign. Pete _____ them with him so that he can read them first.
                        take

He _____ the lawyer that he _____ the papers back next
        tell   send

week. After he finishes with his lawyer, he _____ downtown and
                                                return

_____ his car at the garage. By this time it _____ late
        pick up   be

afternoon. He _____ to the airport to pick up a friend who is coming from
                hurry

Haiti.

He _____ his friend out to dinner. They _____
        take   talk

about old times. They _____ a pleasant evening together. Pete
                            spend

_____ sorry that he decided to see his friend again after all these years.
        be (neg.)

ACTIVITY B   Below are *questions* and *answers* about the story, "Pete's Day." On each line at the left, finish the *question* that goes with the answer.

Questions   **Answers**

1. *Will* _____ ?   No, he won't.

2. *Will* _____ ?   Yes, he will.

3. *When* _____ ?   In the morning.

4. *Why* _____ ?   Because she is an old woman.

5. *When* _____ ?   Later in the afternoon.

6. *Who* _____ ?   His lawyer.

7. *How* _____ ?   By train.

8. *Where* _____ ?   To the airport.

9. *What* _____ ?   Talk about old times.

10. *Will* _____ ?   Yes, they will.

The Homemaker

ACTIVITY A   Look at the picture on page 74. Then read the story below. Fill in the blanks with the *future tense* form of each verb. Where you see _____ write the negative form of the verb.
                                                                    (neg.)

This little girl _____ with ideas about life that are different from those
                        grow up

her grandparents had. She _____ that women must stay home and that
                              think (neg.)

men must go out to work. She _____ that men and women can do many
                                  understand

different things. If she wants to be a wife and mother, she _____ and
                                                                    get married

_____ children. If she wants to have a career, she _____
            have   finish

her education and _____ for a job. If she wants to have both a family and a
                          look

career, she _____ a man who _____ her needs and
                    marry   recognize

_____ her meet them. They _____ this before they get
        help   discuss

married. They _____ together how to work and have a family, and they
                        plan

_____ the responsibilities. They _____ unpleasant
            share   "dump" (neg.)

chores on each other.

When this little girl grows up, she _____ wherever she wants to. She
                                          live

_____ the things she wants in life, and she _____ any
        give up (neg.)   have (neg.)

regrets.

ACTIVITY B   Below are *answers* about the story, "The Homemaker." On each line at the left, write a *question* that goes with the answer.

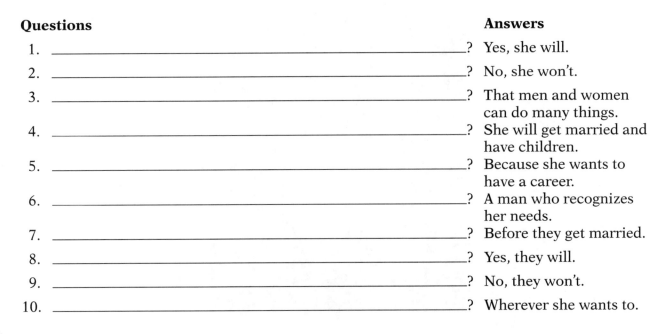

Questions	Answers
1. _____?	Yes, she will.
2. _____?	No, she won't.
3. _____?	That men and women can do many things.
4. _____?	She will get married and have children.
5. _____?	Because she wants to have a career.
6. _____?	A man who recognizes her needs.
7. _____?	Before they get married.
8. _____?	Yes, they will.
9. _____?	No, they won't.
10. _____?	Wherever she wants to.

104

The Football Game

ACTIVITY   Read the story below and fill in the blanks with the *present continuous* form of each verb. Where you see _____ write the negative form of the verb.
(neg.)

Right now I _____ a football game on television. Two good teams
watch

_____. One team _____, 7–0. The other team
play   win

_____ any points. Now two players _____. The referee
get (neg.)   fight

_____ to break it up. The referee _____ a good job.
try   do (neg.)

The fans _____ their team will win.
hope

A Letter

ACTIVITY   Read the letter below and fill in the blanks with the *present continuous* form of each verb. Check the answers with the letter on p. 44.

888 Beach Avenue
Miami, Florida
October 15, 1994

Dear Ricardo,

I _____ on a bench in my neighborhood park and
sit

_____ the beautiful fall weather here. The wind _____,
enjoy   blow

and some leaves _____. I _____ to college now and I
fall   go

_____ English. I _____ also _____
study   work

part-time as an elevator operator.

I _____ now _____ an apartment with my brother
share

Tony and his wife Sara. He _____ in a factory, and she
work

_____ to school. Together we _____ up the apartment.
go   fix

Tony and Sara _____ to go back home for a visit at Christmas, but I
plan

_____ in the city to work.
stay

_____ you still _____ to school? What
go

_____ you _____ to do at Christmas? Write to me soon.
go

Your friend,
Nelson

The Tube Boob

ACTIVITY   Look at the picture on page 46. Then read the story below. Fill in the blanks with the ***present continuous*** form of each verb. Where you see _____ write the negative form of the verb.
(neg.)

    This is the living room of an apartment. There _____ television sets

_____ all around the room. An ashtray _____ on one
stand   rest

television set, an empty coffee cup on another. One television set _____ on
lie

the coffee table and others _____ on the floor. There are even TV sets on
rest

top of TV sets. But they _____.
work (neg.)

    There are three people in the apartment: Ed; Ed's wife, Mabel; and her friend, Maryanne.

Ed _____ another TV set into the apartment. Mabel and Maryanne
carry

_____ next to each other. Mabel _____ to Maryanne.
sit   talk

Ed _____ a long cigar. Mabel _____ but Maryanne
smoke   smile

_____. She _____ to figure out what
smile (neg.)   try

_____ on. Ed _____ anything to Mabel, but he doesn't
go   say (neg.)

have to. Mabel understands what _____ and she _____
happen   begin

to explain the situation to Maryanne. What do you think she _____?
say

Barroom Brawl

ACTIVITY   Look at the picture on page 47. Then read the story below. Fill in the blanks with the *present continuous* form of each verb. Where you see _____ write the negative form.   (neg.)

This incident _____ place in a bar. All the patrons of the bar
                          take

_____ a fight. They _____ anything. They
        have   say (neg.)

_____ just _____. One of the patrons
                              brawl

_____ back with his elbows on the bar. The man in front of him
        lean

_____ him with his right hand and _____ to hit him
        grab   threaten
with the left.

  Behind them a man and a woman _____. The woman
                                              fight

_____ her handbag and _____ to hit him. The man
        swing   try

_____ one of his hands and _____ to defend himself.
        lift   hope
He probably _____ to hit the woman.
                  go (neg.)

  To the right of the woman with the handbag, two men _____ each
                                                            hit
other. One of the men _____ the other one in the jaw. The man who
                              punch

_____ punched _____ over backward. His hat
        be   fall

_____ off his head.
        drop

  In front of them, two more men _____. One _____
                                        struggle   lie
on his back on the floor. The other _____ on top of him. Their hats
                                          sit

_____ on the floor. Next to them, another couple of men
        rest

_____. One _____ the other. They
        battle   strangle

_____ at each other. While all of this _____ on, the
        glare   go
bartenders _____ next to each other behind the bar and
                  stand

_____. They _____ the fight. One
        talk   stop (neg.)

_____ the other how the fight started. What _____ he
        tell

_____?
        say

Looking out the Window

ACTIVITY   Read the story below and fill in the blanks with the ***present continuous*** form of each verb. Where you see _____ write the negative form of the verb.
                                                                                    (neg.)

I _____ in my room and _____ out the window. A
                  sit   look

young couple _____ by. They _____ to each other. An
                          walk   talk (neg.)

old man _____ by. He _____ a heavy package. Here
                  limp   carry

comes a photographer. He _____ along a camera case and a tripod. He
                                       drag

_____ pictures. Here comes a man who _____ a pink
        take (neg.)   wear

hat. Cars and taxis _____ down the street. Now they
                                 drive

_____ for a red light. The light _____ green and they
        stop   turn

_____ again. It _____ but the cars' windshield wipers
        start   rain

_____. It _____ to get dark. I _____
        move (neg.)   begin   try

to work but my daughter _____ in the next room with a friend. They
                                     play

_____ quiet. Now I _____ hungry. I
        be (neg.)   get

_____ work and _____ to eat.
        quit   go

The Teacher's View

ACTIVITY A   Read the story below and fill in the blanks with the *present continuous* form of each verb. Where you see _____ write the negative form of the verb.
(neg.)

I _____ in front of the class. The students _____.
sit   work

They _____ a composition. Well, some of them _____
write   do

it, but others _____ just _____. Some students
laugh

_____ anything. They _____ into space and
do (neg.)   stare

_____ dumb. Maybe they _____. Maybe they
look   try (neg.)

_____. Some _____ to class at all. Freddy
sleep   come (neg.)

_____. Charlie _____ either. The others
fail   pass (neg.)

_____ to pass. I _____ forward to the summer
hope   look

vacation.

ACTIVITY B   Below are *answers* about the story, "The Teacher's View." On each line at the left, write a *question* that goes with the answer.

Questions   **Answers**

1. _____ ?   In front of the class.

2. _____ ?   Yes, they are.

3. _____ ?   A composition.

4. _____ ?   Just laughing.

5. _____ ?   Staring into space.

6. _____ ?   Maybe.

7. _____ ?   Freddy.

8. _____ ?   No, he isn't.

9. _____ ?   Pass.

10. _____ ?   The summer vacation.

Traffic Reporter

ACTIVITY A   Read the story below and fill in the blanks with the *present continuous* form of each verb. Where you see _____ write the negative form of the verb.
(neg.)

This is your WINS traffic reporter. I _____ in helicopter 1010, and
fly

right now I _____ over the West Side Highway. Traffic
go

_____ slowly south, but all vehicles _____ at normal
move   drive

speed going north. The George Washington Bridge _____ a heavy load at
carry

this moment, so if you _____ to get into New York quickly, we
try

_____ you to use the Lincoln Tunnel. Traffic _____
advise   make (neg.)

good time on the FDR Drive south, and it _____ over the 59th Street
crawl

Bridge. Cars _____ now at the entrance to the Holland Tunnel because of a
stop

stalled vehicle in the left lane. It _____ to rain now but it
begin

_____ traffic. Traffic still _____ up at the Brooklyn-
affect (neg.)   clear (neg.)

Battery Tunnel, but it _____ to move on the Brooklyn Bridge. This has
start

been your WINS traffic reporter, and I _____ off now.
sign

ACTIVITY B   Below are *answers* about the story, "Traffic Reporter." On each line at the left, write a *question* that goes with the answer.

Questions	Answers
1. _____?	A helicopter.
2. _____?	Over the West Side Highway.
3. _____?	Slowly going south and at normal speed going north.
4. _____?	The George Washington Bridge.
5. _____?	The Lincoln Tunnel.
6. _____?	No, it isn't.
7. _____?	Because of a stalled vehicle.
8. _____?	No, it isn't.
9. _____?	Yes, it is.
10. _____?	Signing off.

Summer Plans

ACTIVITY   Read the story below and fill in the blanks with the appropriate form for each verb. Where you see _____ write the negative form of the verb. You will have to use
(neg.)
different tenses in this activity.

Next summer I _____ home. I _____ a little and
            stay   work

_____ a lot. I would _____ to _____
  play   like   go

to Canada for a vacation. Five years ago I _____ in Canada and I
                                           be

_____ it very much. I _____ around a lot and
  enjoy   drive

_____ some wonderful meals. I _____ anywhere last
  eat   can go (neg.)

year, and although now I _____ ready to _____ another
                       be   take

trip, I just _____ enough money. My wife _____ staying
        have (neg.)   mind (neg.)

home either. Her parents _____ to _____ us in July. We
                      come   visit

_____ some time at the beach and _____ to
  spend   go

_____ my parents in Texas.
  visit

Henry and Anita

ACTIVITY   Read each part of the following story. Below each part are *answers*. On each line at the left, write a *question* that goes with the answer about the story. You will have to use **different tenses** throughout this activity.

Henry was born in Italy. He went to high school, but he doesn't have a diploma. He lives in the United States now. He is married to Anita. They were married in 1980.

Henry and Anita have one child named Sofia. Henry works in a store and earns $400 a week. He doesn't like his job. He wants to get a high-school diploma.

Questions   **Answers**

1. _____? Italy.

2. _____? Yes, he did.

3. _____? No, he doesn't.

4. _____? In the United States.

5. _____? Anita.

6. _____? In 1980.

7. _____? One child.

8. _____? Sofia.

9. _____? In a store.

10. _____? $400 a week.

Now Henry is attending school at night. He isn't wasting his time. He is studying hard. He and his wife are saving their money. They are planning to buy a house in the future. They will move to the suburbs. Henry will get a different job. Anita will go back to school and get a diploma also. Then she will get a job. They will have a happy life.

Questions   **Answers**

11. _____? Yes, he is.

12. _____? No, he isn't.

13. _____? Studying hard.

14. _____? Saving their money.

15. _____? Buy a house.

16. _____? To the suburbs.

17. _____? Yes, he will.

John's Story

ACTIVITY A   Read the story below and fill in the blanks with the appropriate form for each verb. Where you see _____ write the negative form of the verb. You will have to use
(neg.)
different tenses in this activity.

Last week John _____ two films and a show. He
see

_____ dinner with a friend. He _____ a lot of
have   watch

television. He _____ like doing much work. He _____
feel (neg.)   fall

asleep every night.

This week he _____ much better. Although he
look

_____ his job, he _____ any trouble doing his work. He
like (neg.)   have (neg.)

_____ full of energy. He _____ to work. He
be   walk

_____ to bed early.
go (neg.)

Next week he _____ to get another job. He _____
try   look

in the newspapers and _____ for interviews. He _____
go   be (neg.)

lazy. He _____ to dinners and shows. His friends
go (neg.)

_____ proud of him. He _____.
be   succeed

ACTIVITY B   Below are *answers* to "John's Story." On each line at the left, write a *question* that goes with the answer. You will have to use **different tenses** in this activity.

Questions	**Answers**
1. _____?	Two films and a show.
2. _____?	Last week.
3. _____?	No, he didn't.
4. _____?	Yes, he did.
5. _____?	No, he doesn't.
6. _____?	Yes, he is.
7. _____?	He walks.
8. _____?	Next week.
9. _____?	In the newspapers.
10. _____?	No, he won't.

Picture Story 1 Revisited

ACTIVITY   Form a group of three or four people. Look at the picture on page 71. Read the sentences below describing the picture, and fill in each blank with the *preposition* that you and your group *agree on*. Choose from the list below.

Prepositions

in	to	about	through
on	next to	between	against
at	opposite	behind	
with	across from	under	
of	around	outside	

Think of a good title for the picture. Write it on the line below.

(Title) _____

1. The setting for this cartoon is a typical living room of an apartment _____ a large building _____ a big city.

2. The apartment is _____ the first or second floor _____ the building.

3. _____ the windows, we can see other apartment buildings.

4. _____ the room there are two couches _____ each other.

5. There is a coffee table _____ the two couches.

6. _____ the coffee table there are some flowers _____ a vase and an ashtray.

7. There are some pictures _____ the walls.

8. There is a large plant _____ one picture, and there are some bookshelves _____ all the pictures.

9. There is a lamp _____ one of the couches.

10. There are four average-looking middle-aged people _____ the room and one weird-looking person _____ the room.

11. A dark-haired man _____ glasses is sitting _____ one couch.

12. He has a pipe _____ his mouth and a smile _____ his face.

13. He is holding a drink _____ his hand.

14. He is probably the husband _____ the woman _____ the hostess gown, who is holding a tray _____ some crackers and cheese _____ it.

15. She is the hostess and her husband is the host.

16. She has curly hair and a thin, pointed nose.

17. The woman is serving hors d'oeuvres _____ a man and woman who are sitting _____ the couch that is _____ their host.

18. The woman's arm is resting _____ the arm _____ the couch.

19. Her legs are crossed, and she is balancing a cocktail glass _____ her lap.

20. She is wearing a dark dress _____ a polka-dot scarf _____ her neck.

21. Her companion is sitting _____ her.

22. He is holding a drink _____ his left hand.

23. Both _____ them are looking _____ the hostess.

24. They have worried, puzzled expressions _____ their faces.

25. They are probably wondering _____ the strange-looking sight _____ the window.

26. A rather heavy, bald man is standing _____ a ladder, which is leaning _____ the window.

27. He is wearing a mask _____ angry-looking eyes and big teeth.

28. His big hands are _____ his head with the thumbs stuck _____ his ears, and he is waving his hands as if he is trying to scare the guests.

29. But the hostess does not seem to be worried.

30. She is smiling and saying something _____ her guests.

31. Maybe she is talking about the man, and maybe she isn't. What do you think she is saying? Put her words here:

    " _____

    _____."

Chin's Fruit Store

ACTIVITY   Fill in each blank below with the correct *pronoun* from the list.

Pronouns

Subject	Object	Possessive Adjectives	Reflexive
I	me	my	myself
you	you	your	yourself
he	him	his	himself
she	her	her	herself
it	it	its	itself
we	us	our	ourselves
they	them	their	themselves

Micky Chin owns a fruit store on Main Street. _____ and _____ wife,

Laura, and _____ son, David, work in the store every day of the week. _____

work very hard. Micky goes to the fruit and vegetable market by _____ early each

morning to buy what _____ needs. Laura opens the store at seven. _____

arranges the merchandise and gets ready for the early morning customers. _____

always smiles and talks to _____. The customers smile back at _____. Laura

works by _____ until 8 o'clock. Then _____ mother comes to help. Micky

arrives with the produce by 8:30, and the three of _____ arrange _____ on the

stalls and shelves. _____ do a lot of business in the morning and also late in the

afternoon. David arrives from school about 2 P.M., and Micky tells _____ what to do.

Laura and _____ mother go home at 7 P.M., and Micky and _____ son stay by

_____. _____ close the store at midnight.

_____ fruit store is very successful. When Micky came from Korea five years ago

with _____ family, _____ had very little money. Now _____ is doing

very well. Micky says, "_____ family and _____ work very hard. _____

don't have much time to relax and enjoy _____. But soon _____ will hire some

people to help _____, and _____ lives will be easier. This country has been

good to _____. If you work hard and help _____, _____ dreams can

come true."

Review Exercise 1

Pronouns: he, she, him, her, his, her, they, them, their
Prepositions: at, on, in, for, of, to, from, with

A. In each space below, fill in the correct *preposition* from the list above.

Mary was born _____ Ohio _____ 5 P.M. _____ January 21, 1965. She lived _____ her parents and one sister named Janice. They lived _____ 221 Columbus Avenue. Later they lived _____ Marion Street. However, she spent most _____ her childhood _____ Latin America because her father was _____ the construction business and he was building highways. Mary and her sister went _____ private schools and they got a very good education. _____ course, they both spoke Spanish fluently.

B. In each space below, fill in the correct *pronoun* from the list above.

Mary had dark hair and a very pretty face. _____ eyes were brown and large and _____ teeth were white and even. _____ always weighed too much, though, and didn't have many boyfriends. _____ sister Janice, on the other hand, was slender and blonde and very lovely. All the boys liked _____, and _____ used to go out on a lot of dates.

When Mary finished high school, _____ parents moved back to the United States and _____ went to college. _____ studied languages and was a very good student. _____ didn't have many dates in college either and _____ life wasn't so happy. But _____ had a very pleasant personality, and people liked _____ very much.

C. Fill in the correct *prepositions*.

When Mary graduated _____ college, she applied _____ a job _____ Washington working _____ the government. She went _____ Washington _____ June 1986. _____ Washington she met three young women who were also just starting to work _____ her agency, and they decided to share a house. One _____ the women was _____ New Jersey, and she had a friend named Richard who was also working there. Mary met Richard and fell _____ love _____ him.

D. Fill in the correct *prepositions* (prep.) and *pronouns* (pron.).

Richard liked Mary. _____ went out together _____ three months and had a very
  (pron.)   (prep.)
good time. _____ the end _____ three months, the agency told Mary that _____ was
         (prep.)   (prep.)   (pron.)
going to send _____ _____ the Philippines. _____ told Richard that _____
            (pron.) (prep.)   (pron.)   (pron.)
wouldn't go if _____ didn't want _____ to, but _____ told _____ to go. _____
            (pron.)   (pron.)   (pron.)   (pron.)   (pron.)
planned to go back _____ New Jersey and work _____ _____ father's business.
                 (prep.)   (prep.) (pron.)

E. Fill in the correct *pronouns.*

_____ last night together was very romantic for _____. _____ went out to a

good French restaurant and then _____ took _____ back to _____ apartment for

champagne. _____ promised _____ would write to each other, and _____ gave

_____ a music box that played one of _____ favorite songs, "La Mer." _____ gave

_____ a book of love poems. _____ both cried when _____ said goodbye.

F. Fill in the blanks with the correct form of the verb in the *past tense.* Where you see
_____ write the negative form of the verb.
  (neg.)

Two weeks after Mary _____ in Manila, she _____
                          arrive   meet
Tony. A colleague at the American embassy, where she _____,
                                                            work
_____ her to a little bar in the old part of the city. Tony
     take
_____ playing guitar with a small band, and throughout the evening he
     be
_____ at her and _____ to be playing just for her. Mary
     smile   seem
_____ drinking rum-and-cokes and feeling sorry for herself. She
     keep
_____ Richard very much. During a break, Tony _____
     miss   come
to her table and _____ if he _____ play a song for her.
                      ask   can
She _____ him to play "La Mer." He _____ it and she
          tell   play
_____.
     cry
A week later, Mary _____ back alone to the bar. When Tony
                          go
_____ her, he _____ "La Mer." Later he
     see   sing
_____ down with her and _____ her a drink that she
     sit   buy
never _____ before _____ a Mai Tai. She
            have   call

118

_____ it very much. She also _____ to like Tony. Soon
                like   start
she _____ going to the bar almost every night, and after a while Tony
        be
_____ playing "La Mer" and _____ playing his favorite
      stop   start
song, "El Reloj." Then they _____ out together. Although Mary
                                      go
_____ Richard, she _____ in love with Tony.
  forget (neg.)   fall
Tony _____ very nice to her, but they _____ much
            be   have (neg.)
time together; they only _____ each other during the week. It
                                see
_____ to her; she _____ to marry him.
  matter (neg.)   want
    After Mary had been in Manila for six months, she _____ out she
                                                           find
_____ pregnant. When she _____ Tony, he
      be   tell
_____ he _____ marry her because he
    say   can (neg.)
_____ already married. Mary _____ what to do. She
      be   know (neg.)
_____ of killing herself. She _____ of having an
    think   think
abortion. But then she finally _____ to keep the baby and go back home.
                                      decide

G.   Fill in the blanks with the correct form of the verb in the *present continuous*. Where
you see _____ write the negative form of the verb.
          (neg.)
    Now Mary _____ in Virginia just outside Washington. She
                    live
_____ still _____ for the government and
                          work
_____ to be a good mother to her little girl Kay. Kay is two years old, and
    try
she _____ and _____. Kay _____ to
        walk   talk   go
nursery school. Mary _____ a lot of responsibility She
                            carry
_____ herself and her daughter by working all day, and she
    support
_____ care of Kay at night. Mary _____ out on dates
    take   go (neg.)
but she has friends. They _____ good to her, and they
                                be
_____ for a nice man for her to go out with. But they
    look
_____ any luck. There is only one bright spot in her life. She
  have (neg.)
_____ to Richard.
    write

H. Fill in the blanks with the correct form of the verb in the *simple present.*

Richard still _____ in New Jersey and _____ for his
            live   work
father. He _____ a lot of money. He _____ married.
              make   be (neg.)
He _____ now he _____ ready to get married. That
     think   be
_____ why he _____ to Mary. He
      be   write
_____ that she _____ a little girl. He
   mind (neg.)   have
_____ to see them both.
      want

Mary's friends _____ she should see him again. They
                   think (neg.)
_____ he _____ a good man. They
      say   be (neg.)
_____ her he _____ to be the right person for her. They
     tell   seem (neg.)
_____ her to find someone else. They _____ afraid she
      want   be
will get hurt again. They _____ questions about him, but Mary
                               have
_____ those questions. She _____ happy memories of
  have (neg.)   have
her time with Richard. She _____ to see him soon.
                                hope

Review Exercise 2

A. Fill in the correct *prepositions.*

Denise Graves was born _____ March 24, 1988 _____ Cleveland, Ohio. Until she was two-and-a-half, she lived _____ her parents and two sisters _____ 338 W. Bellevue Street. _____ 10 o'clock _____ the morning, _____ a Saturday _____ September 1990, she was kidnapped by Harold Gross while she was playing _____ the backyard _____ her house. Gross took the girl _____ his parents who lived _____ a farm _____ Buffalo, NY and told them that she was his child. Gross had a brother named Daniel, who lived _____ the same street as the Graves family.

B. Fill in the correct *pronouns.*

Right after the kidnapping, Mr. Graves, the girl's father, went on television to ask for _____ daughter's return. _____ begged the kidnapper to bring _____ back. _____ said that _____ was not healthy and that _____ needed medicine. Mr. and Mrs. Graves were very upset. _____ offered a reward of $10,000 for the return of _____ daughter. Many people called _____ to give advice. Mrs. Graves thought _____ would never see _____ daughter again. Mr. Graves was so upset _____ killed himself. The police found _____ dead in _____ garage near the tailpipe of _____ automobile. _____ said _____ died of carbon monoxide poisoning.

C. Fill in the blanks with the correct form of the verb in the *past tense.*

Two years later, Daniel Gross _____ Denise and

see

_____ the police. He _____ he

call   *say*

_____ her because he had been a friend of the girl's father. Mr. and Mrs.

know

Gross, who were taking care of Denise, _____ arrested. The Cleveland

             be

police _____ Mrs. Graves to Buffalo, and she _____ her

      take   *identify*

daughter. When the mother _____ at the girl, she _____

                    look   *fall*

down and _____. Then she _____ to her and

        scream   *run*

_____ her. She _____ crying when the little girl

  hug   *start*

_____ her. Mrs. Graves _____ Denise back to Cleveland
  recognize (neg.)   bring

but the girl _____ her own name. The mother, who had just married again,
           remember (neg.)

_____ when reporters _____ her how she
  cry   ask

_____. "I never _____ hoping I
  feel   stop

_____ see her again," she _____. She
  will   reply

_____ the reporters that she _____ angry with the
  tell   be (neg.)

kidnapper, but Denise's sisters _____ that they _____ to
                    shout   want

kill him.

D. Fill in the blanks with the correct form of the verb in the **present tense.**

Now the little girl _____ home with her family. She
                   be

_____ her sisters and she _____ her new father, but she
  know   like

_____ her real father. The sisters _____ happy to have
  remember (neg.)   be

her back, and they _____ good care of her. The mother
              take

_____, "I _____ so happy. I _____
  say   be   know (neg.)

what to do first. I _____. I _____ going to lose her
           can think (neg.)   be (neg.)

again."

Denise _____ blond hair and a light complexion.
        have

"_____ me Denise," she _____ her mother because she
  call (neg.)   tell

_____ her name _____ Susan. The mother
  think   be

_____, "We _____. We _____ her
  say   compromise   call

Susan Denise."

SECTION SEVEN

Grammar Study and Practice

The Article *an*

STUDY   The article *a* changes to *an* in front of words that begin with *a, e, i, o,* and *u*. *An* is also used in front of words that begin with *h* when the *h* is *not* pronounced (for example, *honest, hour,* and *honor*).

Example:

INCORRECT: English is **a i**nternational language.
CORRECT: English is **an i**nternational language.

PRACTICE   Correct each sentence and then rewrite it.

Example: Her daughter was in ~~a~~ *an* orphanage.

    Her daughter was in an orphanage.

1. I felt like a ant in front of a elephant.

2. She had a unhappy marriage.

3. You are very intelligent, so make a intelligent decision.

4. He plans to work for a important company.

5. We love them because they gave us a education.

6. Last year he had a experience traveling to another country.

7. I was working with people who formed a association.

8. Three years ago she had a argument with her friend.

9. English is a important language for me.

10. He lives with a old lady.

The Plural of Nouns

STUDY   Words such as *all, many, most of, some, a lot of, a few,* and *a couple of* indicate plural when followed by a **countable noun.** The countable noun must be in the **plural form.**

Example:

INCORRECT: *All* her ***brother*** worked in the fields.
CORRECT: *All* her ***brothers*** worked in the fields.

PRACTICE   Correct each sentence and then rewrite it.

Example: She spent a few ~~minute~~ *minutes* there.

She spent a few minutes there.

1. My mother did most of the thing in the house.

   _____

2. When I am speaking English, I make many mistake.

   _____

3. He likes all kind of music.

   _____

4. In the class I have a lot of friend.

   _____

5. I'm trying to learn to write many composition.

   _____

6. In our society some teenager don't obey their parents.

   _____

7. All their house looked beautiful.

   _____

8. There are a lot of opportunity for an education.

   _____

9. I think that God has many surprise for you.

   _____

10. I dreamed about many different thing.

    _____

Subject–Verb Agreement

STUDY   There must be agreement between the **subject** and **verb**. A **singular subject** (3rd person) requires the use of *is, has,* or *was*. A **plural subject** requires the use of *are, have,* or *were*.

Examples:

A. INCORRECT: Her **husband have** a good job.
   CORRECT: Her **husband has** a good job.

B. INCORRECT: The **subways is** unsafe and dangerous.
   CORRECT: The **subways are** unsafe and dangerous.

PRACTICE   Correct each sentence and then rewrite it.

Example: The college ~~have~~ *has* a beautiful campus.

The college has a beautiful campus.

Note: Some of the sentences below can be changed to either singular or plural.

1. The class were very interesting all the time.

   _____

2. All these conflicts is causing me many problems.

   _____

3. This city have so many people from different countries.

   _____

4. The building are old and in bad condition.

   _____

5. The customer were very angry with her.

   _____

6. This situation have taught me to be more responsible to myself.

   _____

7. She have a very strong character.

   _____

8. My life have changed so much I can't believe it.

   _____

9. The people is worried about their jobs.

   _____

10. The student were studying for the exam.

Indicating Possession with 's

STUDY   Use *'s* to indicate possession.

Example:

INCORRECT: **David** parents were very poor.
CORRECT: **David's** parents were very poor.

PRACTICE   Correct each sentence and then rewrite it.

Example: I want to talk to Maria⎵brother.
                                    ('s)

  I want to talk to Maria's brother.

1. I had a big problem in my sister house.

    _____

2. I went to my grandmother bed and talked to her.

    _____

3. Fatima life was controlled by her mother-in-law.

    _____

4. When I saw that, I ran to my aunt house.

    _____

5. My boyfriend cousin is coming to pick me up.

    _____

6. They decided to talk with Luisa mother.

    _____

7. She has a lot of feelings about women rights.

    _____

8. It is difficult to understand Edward speech.

    _____

9. She felt better after she left her mother house.

    _____

10. Does anybody know who has Teresa book?

    _____

The Subject Pronoun *it*

STUDY   When *is* or *was* is followed by words such as *difficult, hard, easy, important, dangerous, nice, good, comfortable,* and so on, you must put *it* before *is* or *was.*

Example:

INCORRECT: She likes the neighborhood because **is nice.**
CORRECT: She likes the neighborhood because **it is nice.**

PRACTICE   Correct each sentence and then rewrite it.

Example: At first ∧was difficult for me to find a job.
                                it

At first it was difficult for me to find a job.

1. I think is very important to know that.

_____

2. If you know English, is easier for you to find a job.

_____

3. She likes her apartment because is comfortable.

_____

4. Sometimes is very difficult to get some medicine.

_____

5. In the winter is dangerous for my health.

_____

6. Now is too late because he is dead.

_____

7. I think that is hard to take care of the children.

_____

8. Is good to visit your family and help them.

_____

9. For me was hard to realize that I was an alcoholic.

_____

10. For Maria is easy to learn English, but for me is hard.

_____

One of

STUDY   *One of* implies that you are writing or talking about *one of* several or many people, places, or things. For example, if you write "I lost *one of my books*," you are indicating that you have several or many books but that you lost *one of them*. The word *books* has to be in the **plural form.**

Example:

INCORRECT: **One of** my **friend** lost his job.
CORRECT: **One of** my **friends** lost his job.

PRACTICE   Correct each sentence and then rewrite it.

Example: One of these ~~boy~~ *boys* is her son.

One of these boys is her son.

1. I was one of the organizer of the group.

    _____

2. Helen was one of the best student in the class.

    _____

3. One of Jose's girlfriend got jealous and called the police.

    _____

4. One of the best college in the country is Yale.

    _____

5. One of the police officer knocked on the door.

    _____

6. My husband invited one of his friend to our house.

    _____

7. One of her brother lived in a small town.

    _____

8. An education is one of the most important thing we can acquire.

    _____

9. He is one of the person who helped me all my life.

    _____

10. She is one of the best teacher in the school.

    _____

This, These; That, Those

STUDY   *This* and *that* are **singular.** They are used with **singular nouns.** *These* and *those* are **plural.** They are used with **plural nouns.**

Examples:

A. INCORRECT: Many of **this people** think that I'm wrong.
   CORRECT: Many of **these people** think that I'm wrong.

B. INCORRECT: All **that experiences** helped me to learn.
   CORRECT: All **those experiences** helped me to learn.

PRACTICE   Correct each sentence and then rewrite it.

Example: All ~~this~~ *these* people depend on me.

   All these people depend on me.

1. I know that this problems are never going to change.

    _____

2. I didn't finish high school because of this obstacles.

    _____

3. That five years helped me to feel proud of myself.

    _____

4. I didn't know that this sweet girls used drugs.

    _____

5. I feel bad because that two people lied to me.

    _____

6. She really didn't consider all that things to be problems.

    _____

7. This landowners hire peasants to work for them.

    _____

8. That economic conditions cause people to suffer.

    _____

9. All this experiences made me feel that I couldn't trust anybody.

    _____

10. That children are getting a good education.

    _____

Everybody, Everyone, Everything; Nobody, Nothing

STUDY   *Everybody, everyone, everything, nobody,* and *nothing* are plural in meaning but **singular** in **grammatical form.** When you use these words, the verb has to agree in **form,** also.

Example:

INCORRECT: **Everyone have** problems at some time or other.
CORRECT: **Everyone has** problems at some time or other.

PRACTICE   Correct each sentence and then rewrite it.

Example: Everybody ~~are~~ *is* worried about the future.

Everybody is worried about the future.

1. Nobody have time for me.

   _____

2. Everything have a purpose in life.

   _____

3. Everyone are invited to the party.

   _____

4. Nobody understand the way to do it.

   _____

5. Everybody have a different opinion.

   _____

6. Everyone need a good friend.

   _____

7. Everything have to be finished soon.

   _____

8. Everyone were drinking too much.

   _____

9. Everybody are waiting for your answer.

   _____

10. Nobody eat the right kind of food.

    _____

Infinitives—Part 1

STUDY   An infinitive consists of *to* and the **base form** of a verb. You must always use the **base form. DO NOT** add *-ed, -s, -ing,* or **irregular past forms** to the infinitive.

Example:

INCORRECT: He began **to walked** away from me.
CORRECT: He began **to walk** away from me.

PRACTICE   Correct each sentence and then rewrite it.

Example: She had to ~~left~~ *leave* school.

 She had to leave school.

1. He tried to stayed at home with my mother.

   _____

2. I'm going to explained what happened to me.

   _____

3. Elvia's mother finally had to left her husband.

   _____

4. I had to worked in a factory for many years.

   _____

5. Somebody told me to applied for financial aid.

   _____

6. My mother decided to sent me to school.

   _____

7. She started to going out with a boy named Samuel.

   _____

8. She decided that they had to separated.

   _____

9. He came to picked me up at eight o'clock.

   _____

10. Robert wants to goes with us.

   _____

Infinitives—Part 2

STUDY   The **infinitive form** consists of *to* and the **base form.** Use the **infinitive form** after *want, need, like, would like, prefer, have,* and *love.*

Example:

INCORRECT: They **want buy** a new car.
CORRECT: They **want to buy** a new car.

PRACTICE   Correct each sentence and then rewrite it.

Example: She needs *to* find a babysitter.

She needs to find a babysitter.

1. We prefer take the bus to school.

   _____

2. I want go back to my country.

   _____

3. He would like get a job.

   _____

4. They love eat Chinese food.

   _____

5. I have call my father tonight.

   _____

6. She wants get married soon.

   _____

7. I need study for the test.

   _____

8. They like go dancing on weekends.

   _____

9. He prefers live in the city.

   _____

10. I would like buy a beautiful house in the country.

   _____

Double Subject

STUDY   It is incorrect to use two subject words with the same verb.

Example:

INCORRECT: My **father he is** a soldier.
CORRECT: My **father is** a soldier.

PRACTICE   Correct each sentence and then rewrite it.

Example: My aunt ~~she~~ is divorced.

My aunt is divorced.
_____

1. My sister Maria, she is a student.

    _____

2. My family and I we are together.

    _____

3. Ana's life it is less difficult now.

    _____

4. Maria and José, they are husband and wife.

    _____

5. He noticed that the boat it wasn't there.

    _____

6. My friend Cesar he was thinking about where to study.

    _____

7. My mother, she is coming to visit me.

    _____

8. Helen and John, they have three children.

    _____

9. He said that the test it was hard.

    _____

10. Margaret's daughter she is sick.

    _____

Past Tense Negative with *didn't*

STUDY   Use the **base form** after *didn't*. **DO NOT** use the past form.

Example:

INCORRECT: She **didn't wanted** to talk to him.
CORRECT: She **didn't want** to talk to him.

PRACTICE   Correct each sentence and then rewrite it.

Example: We didn't ~~had~~ *have* enough money.

We didn't have enough money.

1. I didn't wanted to think about that.

    _____

2. He didn't went to the party.

    _____

3. When I asked her about it, she didn't answered me.

    _____

4. I didn't knew the answer to the question.

    _____

5. I didn't liked the way he treated me.

    _____

6. They didn't left work until 6:00.

    _____

7. He didn't wanted anyone to see him crying.

    _____

8. She didn't said anything to him about it.

    _____

9. I didn't believed her explanation.

    _____

10. I didn't finished the homework yet.

    _____